MEET IT, GREET IT, AND DEFEAT IT

DISCARD

The Biography of Frances E. Williams, Actress/Activist

BY

Anna Christian

Published by
Milligan Books

Published and Distributed by:
Milligan Books
1425 W. Manchester Blvd., Suite B,
Los Angeles, California 90047
First Printing, April, 1999
10 9 8 7 6 5 4 3 2 1

ISBN: 1-881524-47-7
Library of Congress
Cataloging in Publication Division
Library Of Congress Catalog
Card Number preassigned : 99-093100

Cover Designed by Icehill UltraMedia Creations

Formatted by Black Butterfly Press

Printed in the United States of America

In loving memory

of my father and mother

Elte and Pauline Faulkner

CONTENTS

ACKNOWLEDGEMENTS

I am deeply indebted to the following people for their advice, encouragement and support. Wendall Collins, Saundra Sharp, Shakeh Asfaw, and Bill Smith who read my earlier manuscript and gave me valuable feedback. Jim Haskins who generously shared his material with me, Richard O. Jones who set me on the right track, Dr. Milligan and her staff for all the words of encouragement. A special thanks to all Frances' friends who allowed me into their homes and shared their memories with me, particularly the late Carlton Moss, O'Neal Cannon, Don Wheeldon, Libby Clark, Geri Branton, Admiral Dawson, the late Spencer Morgan, Phyllis Scoby, Marque & Lorna Neal, Lorenzo Torres, Ismael (Smiley) Parras, and Ed Pearle, last but not least my family, Ollie Eubany, my sister, Marcus Christian, my son and J.J. Hodges, my friend.

PREFACE

It was a chilly afternoon in April. Rain had swept the streets the night before, and though the sun shone overhead, dark clouds were threatening. Despite the weather, over 300 people were expected at the memorial service. Two hours before the mourners were due to arrive, the organizers and volunteers hurriedly set up tables in the foyer of the Little Theatre on Southwest College Campus, covering them with the ethnic print cloths Frances would have approved; pinning publicity pictures to backboards covered with muted yellow fabric, advertising flyers and programs from plays she'd produced at her theater; and distributing platters of food across tables - hot wings, sweet and sour meatballs, a variety of breads, vegetable trays, cookies, and cakes, along with vases of daisies, baskets of flowers, and ebony sculptures.

Inside the technicians worked on the sound and lighting, and set designers added finishing touches to the stage - a huge African totem pole in one corner, a grand piano in the other, a giant screen pulled down in the center.

As the hour neared, the lobby began to fill with people - stage and screen actors, singers, musicians, politicians, activists, workers, and just plain folk who had known her, had worked with her, people whose careers she had helped launch, those whose lives she had touched, and some who had never met her but had heard of her. The theater itself became a cauldron, bubbling over with excitement. People who had not seen one another since the last rally, the last event, the last workshop greeted each other as long lost friends, exchanging cards, telephone numbers and promises of future meetings.

1

MEET IT, GREET IT, AND DEFEAT IT

Pulses quickened, flash bulbs popped, as Rosa Parks, flanked by Geri and Leo Branton, made her way through the crowd. State Senator Diane Watson, actors Tim and Daphne Reid, Brock Peters, Esther Rolles and Beah Richards, musician Buddy Collette, and singer Marilyn McCoo, pushed their way through and into the auditorium. Others stood in line at the tables, filling paper plates with food, lingering to gossip and to watch. Gradually the foyer emptied as the people filed into the auditorium to be a part of the celebration - a goodbye party for Frances E. Williams, actress-activist.

I remember the last time I saw her, a few weeks earlier, Christmas time - in the convalescent hospital where she'd been for over a month, her fate no longer in her hands since having a stroke back in September shortly after her 89th birthday. She'd spent almost two months at Centinela Hospital on LaBrea, getting therapy to restore her speech and waiting to see if she would finally be admitted into the Screen Actors' Guild Convalescent Home. In the interim, she was transferred to a convalescent hospital where her health steadily declined.

A week before her death, the nurses said that she was doing a lot better. They told me she had responded when they bathed her. That was a good sign, they said. I almost believed them. But then, I knew Frances. The one thing she wanted most was to go home. She had fought hard - when she was coherent, she had cursed out everyone who came near her, had refused to eat, or to speak to anyone, had pulled IV's from her arm. Finally, realizing she no longer controlled her fate, I think she decided to wage a battle she knew she could win.

I didn't stay more than fifteen minutes, feeling very close to this woman who had encouraged my creative growth and had given me the privilege of knowing her. Frances had shared her life with me and I felt committed to bring her life story to the public - a rich life shared with giants like Paul Robeson, Langston Hughes, James Weldon Johnson, W.E.B. DuBois, and Maya Angelou. Frances, nonetheless, fought much of her life in the crepuscular

2

light of public anonymity.

Months later, as a group of her friends went through her belongings (she had outlived all her relatives) clearing out the house in which she lived for fifty years, I stumbled across a side of Frances of which I'd known little. Sure, I'd spent five years working with her on her autobiography. I was amazed that her memory was so long and vivid. She carried me from her birth in 1905 up to *Frank's Place* in the late 1980's. But it wasn't until sifting through her belongings that I saw another dynamic part of her history that heretofore I'd only glimpsed. Many of her friends and acquaintances knew only one side of Frances. Actors knew only the acting side, activists knew she was an actress yet did not know her religious side. Still, everyone knew who to call whenever action was needed. And whenever Frances was called, she never refused.

She was a born organizer, a lover of children the world over, a fighter of racism wherever it occurred. Yet to some, she was just an old hellraiser. She told me one time, when Roscoe Lee Brown was having difficulty getting the director to listen to him, he threatened to call Frances. After that, he had no more trouble.

At various times in her life, Frances attempted to record her life story, seldom getting past her childhood. Whenever I'd ask her why she hadn't written her memoirs, she'd say she was too busy living to take time out. As we worked on her biography, numerous times we had to stop for Frances to organize a fundraiser for the Aquarius Bookstore which had been burned down in the uprising following the Rodney King verdict, or to sell out a theater performance by Avery Brooks on the life of Paul Robeson for the Paul Robeson Community Center she helped found, or to attend her friends, Paule Marshall's and Maya Angelou's book signings. Being with Frances was an experience in itself. Though she led a full life, it was not without enormous frustration and a heavy price.

Many people have asked "Who is Frances Williams?" This biography hopes to answer that question. A montage of our work together, letters she'd written to others, letters she'd received,

3

notes (she was a copious note maker) from scraps of paper, notebooks, interviews with her friends and acquaintances form this one-dimensional attempt to capture a three-dimensional life.

Moreno Valley, Ca.   Anna Christian
November, 1998

1

THE CURTAIN RISES

"Here I stand all raggedy and dirty.
If you don't come and kiss me,
I'll run like a turkey."
Frances Williams

Shortly after the turn of the century in West Orange, New Jersey, Thomas Alva Edison was working on his latest invention. Not many miles away, in East Orange, a debate raged at the Jones's house - What to name the newest addition to the family? Papa Bill wanted to name his newborn daughter after his mother, whose name was Frances. "No," insisted P.L., who was ten at the time. "She should be named Elizabeth, after Mother." Finally, a compromise was reached. "We'll call her Fanny Lizzie," Papa Bill said to everyone's satisfaction. As soon as Fanny Lizzie was old enough, she abandoned the name for Frankie, then Frances, and finally, Frances E. Williams, Actress/Activist.

William Henry Jones, or Papa Bill, drove a delivery wagon for the A&P grocery store. He was a very gentle loving person, one of 14 brothers and two sisters. Four of his brothers were to lose their lives serving in the First World War. Papa Bill loved Frances very much. Every night he would rock her and sing her to sleep and favor her over her two handsome brothers, Percy Lloyd or P.L. as everyone called him, and Bill.

5

Elizabeth Nelson Jones was a laundress. Though she had only completed the second grade, she was very resourceful. Frances, who loved her mother a great deal, would gaze in fascination as her mother prepared to go out, whether to church or to a show.

Elizabeth was more than attractive; she had style. She could wear a hat and a suit like no one else; she could sing and play the mandolin well, too. Elizabeth would put black stockings in her hair and cover them up to make big poufs, the current rage. When she wanted rosy cheeks, she would take a petal from the flower arrangement on a hat, wet it, and rub it on her cheeks to get the dye for rouge.

On her days off, Elizabeth would go to New York as frequently as she could. Being the youngest, Frances usually accompanied her. Every Thursday, Elizabeth would take her daughter into the city to see wonderful plays such as "The Big Red Shawl" and "In Dahomey." That was Frances's introduction to the theater and to two of the most important black entertainers of the day - Bert Williams and George Walker.

Her grandfather on her father's side had a livery stable with all kinds of carriages and horses. Whenever there was a fancy wedding, Baptism or party in the town, his stables were used. Standing in the entranceway of the different homes, he would announce the arrival of each guest. In a deep rich voice that commanded attention, he'd say, "Mr. and Mrs. So and So have arrived...And here is Mr. So. and So."

Her mother's father, a Cherokee Indian, was a shoe cobbler. Elizabeth would tell Frances stories about her grandfather, whom Frances had never met. Grandfather Nelson owned a shoe shop in New York City. Whenever Elizabeth visited his shop, much to her mother's dismay and his customers' delight, he would teach his daughter how to curse. Then he would put her up on the counter of his shop and let her call his customers "big fat sons-of-bitches" or "big-bellied bastards" and they'd shower her with money.

Grandfather Nelson had a very good singing voice and would stand on the corner and sing to attract crowds for the politicians who would come and make speeches. Between her mother and both grandfathers, Frances was destined to become involved with the arts.

Just two years apart in age, Bill and Frances were very close. Bill had rosy cheeks, deep dimples and long, thick curls that hung down to his shoulders. A great, outgoing personality, Bill was a favorite of everyone. A good athlete, Bill could sing well and tap dance, too, though, in school, he was low scholastically. Throughout their early school years, Mother made Frances do all Bill's homework. Elizabeth would be angry if she didn't; it never occurred to the young girl to refuse. Still, Bill admired his sister greatly. Even when they became adults, he thought she could do anything.

Three members of the family lived on the same street. Aunt Lily, Elizabeth's sister with her three children, Charlie who was the same age as P.L., Orafay, and Oscar. A few years later, Aunt Lily had two more children, Travis and Harriet or Babe, who Frances didn't get to know until both were adults. Also living on that same street was Aunt Effie, Papa Bill's sister. The neighborhood was predominately Italian, and as a result, the first songs and lullabies the children learned were in Italian. On Sunday mornings, Mother would make hot rolls, codfish cakes and a wonderful Italian sauce with onions, garlic, and green peppers.

For reasons unknown to the children, Elizabeth and Papa Bill decided to leave New Jersey and move to Pittsburgh. After putting P.L. in boarding school in Bordentown, N.J., and leaving Bill and Frances with Aunt Lily until they could send for them, Mother and Father went ahead to prepare a new home for the family. A short time later, the two young children were put on a train alone to follow them. No sooner were they on the train to Pittsburgh than P.L. tied sheets to the bedpost, climbed out the window of the dorms, and went to live with Aunt Lily where he stayed until the family could send for him.

The Jones family found a little house in the hills just outside the city of Pittsburgh where many Scots and Irish lived, hills spotted with cows and sheep. However, before they could settle into their new home, Papa Bill died.

7

MEET IT, GREET IT, AND DEFEAT IT

The following entry is from Frances's notebook:

"I was almost 3 years old. Bro. Bill almost 5...Poor mother didn't know what to do - Papa's body was sent back to New Jersey. We were put in an orphanage where I cried every moment and wet the bed every night. At the end of 2 weeks we couldn't stand it any longer. Mother came to apologize. When Mama came to see us, we said that we would both get jobs and work - we could put our money together and eat soup. Meanwhile my older bother had tied sheets to a bed post and escaped from the boarding school, and was staying with relatives back home. Poor Mama had worked so hard to raise the money to pay for P.L. to go to that awful school.

"Mama found a very nice lady in Brushton outside of Pittsburgh where we could all be together - People liked Mama very much. She had a wonderful sense of humor even when things looked insurmountable. She could sing and dance and laugh heartily. We loved her but were afraid of her too. She never whipped us but you always felt that she could end your life if you did wrong. But most important as I think back- she inspired you to tackle a job and do it superbly and she believed in you and trusted you.

"The next year about 1908 - one of the first black policemen in Pittsburgh, Ben Williams fell in love with mother, wooed her by watching over us, housing us, and feeding us things like steak which I never remember eating before. Mother had to get up early to go to work and the policeman would come by to see that we got off to school and the house was all right. We were then living in an upstairs apartment on top of a hill outside of Pittsburgh. There were lots of Italians and Scottish people in the area. I remember billy goats, bagpipes and kilts on Saturday nights and bulls and cows that grazed in big fields.

"Mother and Daddy married and moved us, Bill and me, to Cleveland where Daddy got a job as footman at the May Co. which he kept for 25 years. Every week during those 25 years he brought home fresh cut flowers and cake to mother on Saturdays.

"Mother was still the greatest laundress in the world - We roomed on 43rd street near Cedar Ave. Then we rented a three

8

bedroom apartment at 4210 Cedar Ave. We had a roomer - a Mr. Terry who worked as a pullman porter, one of the better jobs for a colored man in those days. By this time I was five and Bro. Bill was seven and going to school. On the corner of the apartment building in which we lived was a grocery story owned by Mr. Klien. Bro. Bill proved so helpful that Mr. Klien hired him to drive the grocery wagon with horse after school and on Saturdays to deliver the groceries in the neighborhood for 75 cents a week.

"A young couple, who were Mr. Klein's customers, both of whom worked in a defense plant, needed a baby sitter from early morning until 3 p.m. who could give their child her noon meal. I was suggested by Mr. Klien and my brother. I convinced Mama that I could do it. I was tall for my age. I made $3.00 a week for 5 days' work. Mother was only making $1.50 per day and car fare. Mother had promised that we could work and help. This was my chance. That was the year that I was to enroll for kindergarten. But with such a good job, I had to skip it. $7.50 + 3.75 + 3.00= $14.25 per week or $37.00 per month from our combined salaries not counting our stepdad's or the roomer who paid $3.00 per week. The rent as I recall was $28.00 per month. But we saved enough money to send for my older brother. How we sacrificed to get that money together!

"That summer there was a special kind of boat ride picnic up Lake Erie to Buffalo N.Y. and return. They took me to stay with a Mrs. Pembleton, the mother of our neighbor, over the weekend...because I didn't have any good shoes to wear. But no one told me until several years later that they had all gone on a boat ride. Mother felt so guilty she bent over backwards being kind and thoughtful to me the next few weeks.

"(Mrs. P's?) husband was a building constructor and had built his own 4 unit apartment in an almost predominantly Italian community. Next door in the basement lived an Italian man who then owned several buildings and shops on the next main street called Kinsman. As I write this I start squirming and scratching. It seemed for hours that evening we saw this man through the window picking lice out of his head and heard them crack as he killed them. I'd never seen anything like that before. Negroes have dry scalps - so never have any bugs or lice in their hair. After that I would look for them on the children's hair at school.

"There was a graveyard near Mrs. P's home. That's when I learned that gypsies put food on the graves of the dead. I remember saying I wish I had known that some of those days when we were real hungry. There were so many graveyard stories told that night I could hardly go to sleep and in a strange bed that I was so afraid of walking. I used to pray every night 'Now I lay me down to sleep, I pray the Lord my soul to keep. If I should die before I wake, I pray the Lord my soul to take. God bless Mama, Papa, Bill and Percy and all my aunts and relatives I love so well, and please God don't let me wet the bed for Jesus Christ's sake, Amen.'

"Bro. Percy came out. He was ten years older than I. Daddy got him a job wrapping packages at the May Co. Three of us slept in one bed. One at the foot and two at the head - me wetting the bed almost every night.

"After my father died whom I loved dearly - I knew no one else loved me - my brothers just had to have their hair cut and brushed but mine had to be braided everyday. I had one braid on top and two on each side. Mother would get her knee in my back as I sat on the floor in front of her and braid and pull my hair so tightly that I not only looked oriental, but I was cowlicked almost to the center of my head. Then I had two huge buck teeth that projected out of my mouth. No one could convince me that anyone could possibly love me. If you looked at me I cried. In fact, the first nine years of my life I spent in tears.

"But I did stop wetting the bed when I was about seven and going to school. I worked so hard, praying and trying not to - that I started walking in my sleep. We had moved to 70th Street and Euclid Ave. in Cleveland, a very fine apartment house [that] was built by a Mr. Shapiro. He wanted my folks to be janitors of it. It meant free rent and a small amount of cash. Mother could be home with us everyday, at least [she] didn't have to go out to work - But to top it off, Mr. Shapiro decided to name the apt. "Frances" after me. That recognition helped me a great deal.

"My brothers had a back bedroom down the hall - we had our first telephone in that hall. There was a bathroom and kitchen off the hall, then Mother and Dad's room - the dining room(,) and I slept on a new folding brown leather couch in the living room with a three panelled screen around my bed. The entrance door to the apartment was in the dining room and we kept the light on for my older brother. That's why I had to have the screen around my bed.

"All the children on our street went to bed at 7 o'clock. We had to be in bed by 7:30. We not only worked but had chores to do around the apartment. With a room to myself, I wore the library out. I read at least one book a night through the crack of light that came where the panels hung together on the screen. The longer my big brother stayed out, the longer I could read. I was so determined not to wet that beautiful couch that I started walking in my sleep.

"One night while sleep walking, I entered my mother's bedroom, pulled the covers back off my step father's stomach, sat upon it and let go, thinking I was in the bathroom. Suddenly I heard my stepfather who weighed 240 pounds say, 'Jesus Christ, Lizzie! What's happening!' I can't remember ever wetting the bed again after that."

When Frances was nine years old, the doctor diagnosed her with tuberculosis. She had always been so thin that Brother Bill would joke, "We have to feed her muddy water so you won't see through her." The doctor told her parents that she would have to go to the country so that she could get fresh air and milk. The family didn't have money to send her anywhere. Elizabeth answered a newspaper ad for a housekeeper and an upstairs maid for the summer. Frances's job was to be maid and upstairs girl.

In the first month, due to the fresh air, the rich cow's milk and fresh vegetables, Frances gained over twenty pounds. By the end of the summer, when it was time for her to return to school, she was a plump little girl.

2

THE CHURCH

"Wash me and I shall be whiter than
snow."
Frances Williams

One Sunday morning Elizabeth took the family to St. John's AME Church. After several visits, when the minister opened the doors of the church, Frances decided to join. As the choir sang "What a Friend We Have in Jesus," she got up from her seat and started for the front pew. All eyes followed her down the long aisle. When she reached the front, she sat down. Soon after, her mother came up and sat beside her, followed by her brother Bill. After the service, all the people huddled around them and told them what fine children they were and invited them to their Monday evening instruction class which began at 7 p. m.

For three weeks, Bill and Frances went for instructions to learn the AME church doctrine and to study the Bible. About the fourth week, the minister had to go out of town. Since he couldn't be there, the members decided to turn the session into a prayer meeting. The children had never gone to a prayer meeting and really didn't know what it was. Every single person in the class that evening prayed except Bill and Fanny. As each one finished his testimony, Frances felt her stomach tighten. Finally it was their turn. The people all waited for the children to say a prayer. One older woman looked at Frances and said, "You could say 'Jesus Loves You' or something." Another said, "Everybody should be able to say a prayer. I don't care how

13

young you are!" Suddenly they all lambasted the children for not praying. "We were so intimidated and so unhappy and so without knowledge of what to do in that situation that we got up and walked out," Frances said. They never went back to St. John's A.M.E.

Her next experience with the traditional church was much more pleasant. She had always been attracted to ornate rituals and on her first visit to St. Andrew's, a high Episcopal church, she fell in love with the ceremony, the vestments, the lights and candles and decided she wanted to be a part of it.

Along with the elaborate rituals, Frances was drawn to Sister Annamae, a nun who wore a very smart grey tunic that looked as if it had been designed by Dior. Frances joined St. Andrew's, bringing with her the entire family with the exception of her stepfather. The head of the church was Father Southern. His wife's name was Margaret. They had two children, Orin and little Margaret.

No sooner was Frances baptized, that she became immersed in the church, and loved it. She became a member of the choir, attended Sunday School, and quickly rose to Sunday School Teacher and Superintendent, and finally president of the altar guild. She even considered being a nun so that she could wear one of those beautiful tunics!

At St. Andrew's, Frances met a diverse group of people - doctors, dentists, teachers - and occasionally she would see author Charles Chestnutt, though at the time she did not know who he was. She came to know a doctor who had a very fine dancing group that toured the country. Knowing that she was a good dancer, having choreographed dance productions at the Elks, he offered her a very good contract to join his group.

Mother went to the priest for advice. Father Southern and his family were so close to the Williams family that whenever he and his wife went away, their two children stayed at the Williams's home. Father Southern said, "No, I feel she's like my daughter and I don't think she should go." When her mother told her what Father Southern had said, Frances felt betrayed. She decided to quit the church.

One of the church women with whom Frances became close friends was Garnet Atkins. Garnet was stunning and sophisticated and several years older than she. She was about 5'8" and wore custom-made broadcloth suits with a three-quarter length coat. Her husband, Clarence Atkins, whose family was from Winston Salem, North Carolina, was an engineer for the public school system. They had a child, Jean, who Frances describes as being the most beautiful child she'd ever seen with long brown hair, skin like alabaster, and the cutest mouth.

Clarence was a very jealous man. Sometimes he would question Garnet about Frankie. To her friends, Frances was called Frankie. Though he'd met her several times, Clarence never associated the name Frankie with Frances for years.

"Who's this Frankie?" he wanted to know. He followed his wife night after night, days, weeks, months trying to learn who was this person Garnet talked so much about.

One night when Frances came home, her mother and father told her to terminate her friendship with Garnet because she was a married women and she, Frances, was too young to have married friends. And they had heard that Garnet was thinking about getting a divorce and that was not done in the Episcopal church.

"That's all right, " Frances said quietly. "I can't do it tonight, but Monday, I'll find a place to live. Garnet is my friend and I'm going to keep the friendship."

When she went to bed she overheard her mother and stepfather talking. After a while her stepfather came over and knocked on her door. "Kid," he said. "Mother and I talked it over and we decided that if the friendship means that much to you, keep it. We want you to stay home." Frances was amazed to realize that though she was only fourteen years old, her parents knew that if she made a decision to go, she would go.

Garnet and Clarence eventually divorced. Garnet went to New York to study nursing. Whenever Frances went to New York, she stayed with Garnet in her apartment in Harlem. Among Garnet's circle of friends were writer Langston Hughes, singer and actress

Ethel Waters, clairvoyant Ruthie Thompson, and sculptor Zell Ingram whom Garnet later married.

It was at St. Andrew's that Frances became involved in their theatre workshop and hence the beginning of her lifelong profession. The workshop was run by a man named Arthur Spencer. "I thought he was a great actor. I'd never spent that much time around an actor before. He was very able, not just as a great teacher, but also as an actor. He could create atmosphere so that you felt you were right where he was, either that or I had a very vivid imagination. He could create a character and maintain it so that you really felt you were sharing a space with the character that he was. After working with him for a couple of years at the workshop, I heard about the Dumas Dramatic Club on thirty-eighth Street."

3
———

SCHOOL DAYS

Growing up in an Italian neighborhood, spending much of her childhood in an integrated environment, Frances was not overly conscious of racial prejudice, nor did she ever think of herself as being inferior to any of her friends whom she could out-run, out-jump, you name it, she could do it. It wasn't until high school that an incident brought home to her the nature of discrimination.

Brother Bill was a beautiful runner and Frances could run, too. Both were good all-around athletes. While they were in junior high, though they were the only blacks in the school, Bill became captain of every team sport - gymnastics, track, and basketball.

In high school, Bill played football. Because of his enthusiasm and outgoing personality, everyone loved him. Though once again he excelled in sports, he was not chosen to be captain of the team despite the recommendations of his coaches.

Like Bill, Frances was one of the best athletes in the school. However, she wasn't allowed to be a member of the swimming team because the team used the Cleveland Athletic Club to practice, and Blacks were not allowed in the club.

Frances was very unhappy about it and therefore she quit school. Actually, she quit high school five times; it never made any sense to her, she said. Her mother had only gone to the second grade and she didn't know anyone who had gone to high school or college, still she had better jobs than most people she knew.

While in junior high, she worked weekends with her mother and Mr. Naughton, a caterer. While in high school, she had a good paying job at Sherbundy's, an exclusive restaurant on Euclid Ave, which was then a very fancy street.

Each time she quit school, her mother would make her go back. Finally, the principal, Mr. Lowry, told her mother, "Just tell your daughter there's an old saying that says you can cut off your nose to spite your face but you won't look very good."

At the time, school meant little to her because she was surrounded by all she felt she needed. Besides, never having difficulty finding employment, she'd always been an avid reader thanks to her neighbors, the Beardsly sisters, two retired ladies who once ran a finishing school for girls. For cleaning up after their parties, they kept her supplied with beautifully bound books because they knew she loved literature.

An artist friend, with whom she'd take long walks around Cleveland, taught her a lot about watercolor. Across the street lived the conductors of the Cleveland symphony, and down the street lived Noble Sissle's brother. When Sissle came back from the war, he'd come and play music in the courtyard. Life was rich except for the problem with the school athletic team. This upset her greatly.

Sunday mornings, she would take long hikes through the woodlands of Cleveland surrounded by lilac and dogwood trees. "God, this is not fair," she cried as she walked. "If I had a swimming pool of my own, I'd show them."

Cleveland had the first black city councilman in the country, Thomas Fleming. Uncle Tom, as Frances called him, was a big man with a big head, thick black hair, big hands, big feet, beautiful teeth and a gorgeous dark red complexion that reminded her of an Indian. His wife, Lethia, was almost as tall with long gray hair combed back into a bun. She, too, looked like an Indian.

Fleming was very popular and knew how to get things done. Somehow he managed to get a big gymnasium site with playground, Olympic size swimming pool, track and a room for dances, parties, and banquets, and a bath house in the black community. At the time there were very few young black people in the city involved with athletics. Frances had always been active, not only in athletics and in

18

church, but also with the Elks. She had choreographed all the big music and dance productions for the Elks, and she was in a drama group.

One night E. Warren, his niece, came out to her house. She told Frances her uncle wanted to see her. E. Warren and Frances were very good friends. A few years older than Frances, E. Warren lived with her uncle and aunt.

They rode the streetcar over to her uncle's. The Flemings lived in a huge red brick mansion on the other side of town. "Frank," he greeted her. "You know how to swim, hike and do gymnastics." She told him she could travel rings and work the trapeze, too. "How would you like to organize the activities at the gymnasium and swimming pool?" At that time, Frances didn't even know how to say "municipal" yet in three weeks she had the job of director of activities at the Central Avenue Bath House with a good salary, and she was still in high school!

The Central Avenue Bath House, located in the Roaring Third of Cleveland, was situated in a poorer section of the city, with a mixture of Italian and German immigrants and blacks newly up from the South. The Williams family lived far out in the suburbs. Upon learning of Frances's new job, several of the neighbors tried to discourage her mother from letting her take it. One asked her mother, "You aren't going to let your little girl go down there, are you?" She overheard her mother answer, "I've taught her everything I can teach her, and I trust her." That really bolstered her confidence.

After school each afternoon, Frances took the bus to the Central Ave. Bath House in the Roaring Third. There she managed the activities, setting up swimming programs, teaching the young people that came all she knew, and training the drill teams who performed in the Sunday parades.

Two women she helped train at the Central Avenue Bath House were Stella Walsh and Naomi Smith. Stella became one of the first woman officials in the Olympics. Naomi, a beautiful young woman with a straight, gorgeous body, really excelled more than Stella. She could out run everyone, but she never had the opportunities that Stella

19

had. At that time, Blacks were barred from participating in the Olympics. As a result of the training they received at the Bath House, nine of the young people Frances worked with became physical education instructors.

Sometimes when she wasn't busy, Frances would sit by the window, gazing with fascination at the steady flow of foot traffic, thinking about all she'd heard, the cautionary words of her mother and neighbors. She'd study the people coming down the street. If their eyes were red, she'd think naively, "That's what they get for drinking!"

Not all the residents of the community were downtrodden or involved in shady activity, she soon discovered. There were old residents in the Roaring Third who had great dignity. Her friend's father owned a barber shop not too far away from the Center. A resourceful man, every month, he would buy season theater and concert tickets for his seven children so they would all have something of culture.

When she wasn't working, Frances would spend as much time as she could at the barber shop with Dorothy, one of the barber's daughters, who played violin. Years later, Dorothy played in the women's symphony in Cleveland.

One day, they sat down and had a very serious discussion about their future husbands. They decided that they wouldn't get married unless their names could be alliterated. Dorothy married Alex Dupree and became Dorothy Dupree, and Frances married George Ferguson and became Frances Ferguson. Neither marriages lasted more than a year.

Because of her job as activities director at Central Avenue Bath House, her dream of having a swimming pool at her disposal became a reality. To her delight, she invited the swimming team from East High School to the Bath House; thereafter they came every week to swim. In fact, the entire high school athletic team made it their permanent place to practice.

* * * * * *

20

Since she had to work so hard to help support the family financially, Frances missed out on vacations. Many nights, she'd come home and cry. Her first real vacation came one summer when her friend Florence Bundy invited her to go with her and her family to a resort in Idlywild. Every year, they spent their vacation there and this time, with her parents' consent, Frances accompanied them.

Florence's father, Dad Bundy, drove a brand new Ford with open sides. All the way up to the resort, he would spit out one window and it would fly in the other. Frances happened to be sitting right behind him.

The first day at the resort, they went on a hike, and somehow Frances got into some poison ivy and broke out in a rash all over her body. At meals, no one wanted to sit next to her because her face was covered with pimples. Light-skinned, Florence was a stunning blond with blue eyes. The other girls were equally attractive and vying for the eligible young men. It could have been a disaster for Frances had it not been for Florence's mother, Dorothy. She took Frances to the pharmacist who made up a concoction which cleared the rash up.

Once the rash cleared up, Frances took over the place. Determined not to be left out, she invented and organized games like Round Robin. She went horseback riding and dancing. At the end of their three-week stay, Frances had several proposals of marriage.

3

PLAYHOUSE SETTLEMENT

"Do not throw upon the floor the crust you cannot eat
For many little hungry ones would think it quite a treat
A willful waste makes a woeful want
And you will live to say
'Oh, how I wish I had that crust of bread
that once I threw away'"
Frances Williams

In the lower part of Cleveland, settlement houses were established as welfare and community centers to help the poor. Within the Roaring Third section, the community was a mixture of Jewish, Italian and Negro families with Italian immigrants predominating, until Blacks from the South and other parts of the country began moving in. To the east of the Roaring Third was a mostly Jewish settlement. However, the only settlement house in the city at that time that welcomed Blacks was Playhouse Settlement, founded by Russell and Rowena Jelliffe in 1915.

After graduating with their masters' in social work from Oberlin College, which was about thirty-five miles from Cleveland, the Jelliffes came to the Roaring Third and bought two houses on East 38th Street and Central Avenue, one for themselves, and the other, which had once been a funeral parlor, for their projects. They started a playground and lived in a little house in back.

Down the street from the Settlement was the Central Avenue Bath House. After a while, Frances found that working at the Bath

23

House lost some of its fascination. She began to long for something that would challenge her mentally, not just physically. Encouraged by her friend E. Warren, who was in charge of handicrafts at all the playgrounds, Frances began going over to the Settlement playground, organizing games and helping with craft projects.

When the Jelliffes asked her to work for them at the Playhouse Settlement, she eagerly accepted. Her job was to interview incoming students, assign them to an activity group, and handle two clubs. Eventually, she became the Settlement's first resident worker and lived there fourteen years until she left to study theater in the Soviet Union.

Many of Oberlin's graduate students came to Playhouse Settlement as volunteer workers. Among them were curators from the Cleveland museum: artists like Ash Harmon and Marian Bonsteel, whose uncle owned the Bonsteel Theatre in Detroit; high school principal, Hazel Mountain Walker; and young people like Zell Ingram and Langston Hughes.

The Settlement House consisted of four rooms, one of which served as a kindergarten in the day, and at night was a reading and rehearsal room, as well as a place to store their costumes. Another room, the game room, held a pool table. A third room housed the marionette and print shop, while a sixty-seat theater filled the fourth room. Occupying part of the second floor was the art department. Part of the Settlement was for recreational activity for the young, including a children's theater started by Rowena Jelliffe and later, an adult theater.

The Settlement House opened Frances up to a world that would resonate throughout her entire life, shaping her into the actress/ activist she would become. It stimulated her budding curiosity and satisfied her abundant energy. At the Settlement, she became a writer, director, organizer, as well as social worker.

Shortly after Frances began working at Playhouse Settlement, her brother P.L. purchased a house in Oberlin. After working in the post office and at Halley Bros, P.L. felt he just couldn't make enough money to support the family, so he went into the rackets and became one of the most successful numbers man in the Mid-West. Out of his winnings he purchased a beautiful two-story L-shaped wooden home for them in Oberlin. The family called it "the homestead."

Though they wanted Frances to go with them, she refused. She had become very involved with Playhouse Settlement and didn't want to leave. Because she had always been very independent, the family knew they could do nothing to stop her. Therefore, when they moved, she got a room at the Phyllis Wheatley Girls' Home.

Shortly after she became a resident worker, Frances moved first to the house in the back of the playground, where the Jelliffes had lived- they built a home in Shaker Heights, - then into the Settlement House, into an apartment upstairs over the print and marionette shop.

Some weekends, she went home to Oberlin. Other times her mother, Elizabeth, would come down and stay with her a week or so. For a while, Brother Bill lived with her there and worked in some of the productions. When she married, she lived there for almost a year with her first husband, George Ferguson.

Since Frances lived in the same community as her clients, being a resident worker was like an extension of home. She became a part of their family, developing warm relationships with her neighbors. Twice a week, when any of the neighbors made homemade Italian bread, wine from the fig trees that dotted the community, or tomato puree, they shared it with her. Whenever children stayed out late, they almost always came to her apartment, not leaving until she called their parents.

During the Depression, with unemployment soaring, Frances helped develop a children's club and a mothers' club. Both were successful.

"We tried to get as many mothers in the community into the mothers' club including one Italian woman, Mrs. Camarari, who consistently refused to join despite the fact that all her children were involved in clubs and crafts workshops at the Center.

"One day I was at Mrs. Camarai's house to pick up her youngsters. She was busily hanging out sheets on ropes attached to tall wooden poles suspended just high enough not to touch the ground. They soon crisscrossed the yard.

"Just as I turned to go, she yelled. 'Miss Williams, don't go yet. I want to talk to you.' I was delighted because I had been trying to develop a relationship with her so that she could come to the mothers' club.

'I got to tell you about my husband,' she said, taking a clothes pin from her mouth to secure another end of the sheet. 'He no goddamn good for sheet and I think you can help me do something about it.' While I was never able to convince her to become a member of the mothers' club, she helped out whenever we needed her, making food and other things."

Every time Frances went to pick up the mothers and their children, she saw unhappy men at home. After much discussion, she convinced several of them to come down to the Settlement.

The fathers' club was started with seven men. They were taught to read, speak, debate and report on what was happening in the community. In time, the club grew to three hundred, forcing the Settlement to purchase a new building to house them.

To hear the stories these men related was an eye opener for the young woman who had never been further south than New Jersey. For example, Frances learned that a number of these men had come up from the South because of the Ku Klux Klan. Whenever these men would pool their money to buy a cotton gin or any type of business, no sooner did they become successful, then the Klan would see that they failed by lynching or burning them out and doing all sorts of horrible things. After their businesses had been burned down two or three times, the insurance company would tell them they could no longer afford to insure them. Unable to make a living down there, they came North.

Years later, on her first Sunday in Moscow, a big celebration was held for the Stakhanovites, workers who had excelled in their field of work far beyond where it was thought they could. One person honored was from the cotton industry. Frances was asked to speak at a party for this man hosted by a group of writers and theater people. Much of the material for her speech came from what she had learned at the fathers' club.

Among the speakers invited to speak at the club was A. Phillip Randolph. He was in the process of organizing and bringing the pullmen porters into the American Federation of Labor Union. It was a difficult period because though the A.F. of L. wanted an integrated union, they hadn't fought for the black man to a noticeable degree. Randolph, together with the other black workers, decided that in order to be more effective, they had to unify themselves which is what they did, resulting in the successful formation of the Brotherhood of Sleeping Car Porters.

Randolph and Frances became good friends, and it seemed that in whatever city she was performing, she'd run into him. He'd tell people that she was the only actress he'd seen that "when she comes in the door, you know where she's coming from and when she goes out the door, you know where she's going. And nobody can run up and down the stairs like this woman."

Life in the Roaring Third intrigued Frances. One evening, she watched a crowd of black people almost attack a white woman in a car. "I don't know what that woman did, but she fought back almost running them down. Once I stood on the edge of a crowd watching two prostitutes fight over a priest who was one of their customers.

"Because I lived on the premises of the Settlement, whenever I was alone, the Jelliffes provided me with a German Shepherd police dog. In turn, I would have to walk the dog, sometimes at twelve or one a.m. One evening I had walked a couple of blocks when I passed one of the working girls. She smiled at me and said, 'How's tricks up the block? It's really slow down here.' 'It's slow there, too,' I responded."

* * * * * *

27

MEET IT, GREET IT, AND DEFEAT IT

THE GILPIN PLAYERS

"In come a tall coon dressed in yellow
His hair was slicked down with mutton tallow
Said he was the finest coon in town.
I think they called him "Slewfoot Brown"
Oh, as he possum along, did he possum along
Didn't we have a scand'lous time
At the Possum Along Ball."
from "Possum Along"

If work at the Settlement filled Frances's days, the theater consumed her nights. Though she began with the children's theater, writing and directing some of the plays, she also performed in the adult theater with Hazel Mountain Walker, John Marriott, and others.

The sixty-seat theater was always packed. Sustaining tickets sold out the house for a year during which they did six plays, performing every weekend, plays like *Scarlet Sister Mary*, *Cinderella,* and *Stevedore.* (The Plain Dealer Magazine, Sept. 1990, pg. 18-26)

In 1921, Charles Gilpin, who played *Emperor Jones* and was one of the first African American actors on Broadway, came to see their performance. After the show, he came backstage and encouraged the actors to speak in their own voices and make their "little theater" into a real Negro Theater. He gave them fifty dollars towards their cause. To honor him for believing in them, they changed the name from the Dumas Dramatic Club to the Gilpin Players. And in 1925, they performed Ridgeley Torrence's *Granny Maumee*, their first play about black life.

Many well-known people visited, exposing them to some of the best things happening in black life, people like W.E. B. DuBois, Alaine Locke, and Ethel Waters. This tall, long-legged woman wore a raccoon coat that came down to her ankles. After the performance, one evening, Miss Waters came backstage and spoke to the group. Frances watched her walk from her dressing room to the theater door.

Just as she reached it, she turned dramatically and said, "So long, Miss Williams," in a voice that stayed with the young actress for years.

Most of the audience were white, but the number of blacks attending grew when they did *Little Augie*, a play written by Countee Cullen. The community became involved when the actors went through the neighborhood in search of costumes for the plays. They found much in trunks stored away in attics. Though it was a new experience for most of the black people in the community, from that time on, they not only attended the theater, but also participated and contributed.

In 1927, after the theater was remodeled and decorated with African masks and hangings, the name was changed to Karamu House, a Swahili word for central meeting place. With the Jelliffes consent, the young men and women volunteers formed an African Art Club and raised $1500 for Paul Bow Travis to purchase African artifacts from Africa. The collection has since been given to the Cleveland Museum of Art and the Cleveland Historical Society.

Many plays that were first performed elsewhere came to Karamu, but numerous times they performed original ones like Cullen's play Little *Augie*, renamed *House of Flowers* when it was presented on Broadway. When it opened on Broadway, *House of Flowers* launched the careers of Geoffrey Holder, Pearl Bailey, and Carmen DeLavallade.

Frances's brother Bill made his stage debut in that production. In one scene, the characters, dressed in gorgeous costumes, danced a cakewalk. "Bill out cakewalked everybody. How he'd throw that head back, he was beautiful!"

After Katherine Cornell's acclaimed performance in *Scarlet Sister Mary* on Broadway, the Gilpin Players decided to present it. Frances played the lead in this practically one woman show. Her brothers and mother came down from Oberlin to see the play. The first production of *Porgy* took place at Karamu. Frances played Serena, a role Rose McLendon later did on Broadway.

Whenever a black theater group came to town, Karamu was among the first to receive them. When the Broadway cast of *Porgy*, which included Frank Wilson in the title role and Evelyn Ellis as Bess, came to Cleveland, the group went to see it at the Hammond Theatre. Afterwards, they threw a big party for the cast at the Elks.

During the last two weeks of the play, Frances spent a great deal of time with Frank Wilson. The next time *Porgy* came out to Cleveland, Wilson and his wife stayed at Frances's little apartment. During the day, they went for long walks together. He looked so handsome in his beret that Frances soon developed a serious crush on him. She was awed that this man whom she admired so much would pay any attention to her. His wife, realizing it was just a little school girl crush, was "so mature and healthy about it and somehow, I weathered it," said Frances. The three of them remained friends for many years after that.

One summer, the Gilpin Players participated in the city's outdoor opera productions. W.E.B. Du Bois's second wife, Shirley Graham, who was doing her graduate work in theater at Oberlin College, wrote a play that the actors liked so much they suggested she make it into an opera. Shirley's opera was accepted as one of the six operas to be performed that season. Jules Bledsoe, a very talented black man with great ability, was chosen to sing the lead.

The Harlem Renaissance was at its height, and every six weeks while working at the Settlement House, Frances would go to New York with a group of her friends including Marian Wilson, a physical education teacher, Florence Bundy, or sometimes with her friends from Karamu. Prohibition was in full swing; however, nothing stopped them from going to all the nightclubs in the city. Frances went so regularly to one club that when she'd get out of a taxi, the footman would call into the club, "Miss Williams is here. Shake up a ..."

"I was drinking something that had Kahlua in it, a sweet, horrible drink - it was my favorite and I felt very important.

"Ethel Waters was dancing at the Savoy when I took Ash Harmon and two or three graduate students from Oberlin there. I wanted them to really enjoy Harlem. At the door, the doorman said, 'Pardon me, Miss Williams. You may come in but your friends cannot.'

'I beg your pardon?' I said.

'We don't allow whites in here at all.'

'I didn't know that.' After a moment, I turned to my friends, 'Now you know how it feels. I can go in, but you can't. So you folks go on downtown because I'm going in.'

"At other times, I would go up to Ohio to watch Brother Bill play football. He was on the football team at Ohio State University. Frequently, a group of ten or twenty of us would rent a whole train car, take a little piano and a piano player, some liquor and food, and go up to wherever Bill was playing. I would wear my long-haired possum coat with a big chrysanthemum and everyone would have a ball all weekend!"

(She threw back her head and laughed her deep throaty laugh as the memories came flooding back. Then she rubbed her knee which had begun to ache and said, "Let's see if we can't find something to eat.")

* * * * * *

KARAMU HOUSE

Karamu House was one of the few places in Cleveland that provided an outlet for black writers. As a result, Frances was fortunate to meet so many very fine creative people like writer Langston Hughes and artist Zell Ingram. Ingram worked in the arts and crafts department teaching youngsters in the late afternoons after his own classes at the Cleveland School of Arts.

Frances, Langston Hughes and Zell Ingram were like sister and brothers going on hikes, having picnics, and cook-outs together. When Hughes decided to go to Cuba and Haiti, he asked Frances and Zell to accompany him. Frances's family dissuaded her from going. It was one of the few occasions when they succeeded. Langston and Ingram went together. In his autobiography, *The Big Sea*, Hughes chronicles their adventure.

Every March, Zell and Frances would go up to Chippewa

Valley Camp, one of the first integrated summer camps in the country. Frances was director of summer camp. There they would break the ice and go swimming. Ingram became a sculptor, and a good friend of Romaine Bearden, and William Artist. Before going to Guadalahara to live, he came out to Los Angeles and built the entrance to Frances's theater.

Though Langston wrote for the Central High School publication, he needed a place to express himself creatively. There was no place except at Karamu House. He wrote poetry and children's plays, many of which were performed in the theater. Whenever he had problems at Central High, he'd come and tell his friends at Karamu about them. They would sit down and discuss ways of solving them. Russell and Rowena Jelliffe, whose contributions were very valuable in telling them how to solve their problems, were often included.

However, one thing that always disturbed Frances about Russell and Rowena was that from time to time, they would go to New York for several weeks to study theater. They learned many things there, but Frances felt they never shared what they learned with the group; they never encouraged others to go to New York to study. Consequently, although they all wore several hats at Karamu House, what Frances felt she learned about theater was almost accidental.

Rowena Jelliffe directed the adult plays while Russell Jelliffe did most of the technical part of it. Eventually they started to train some of the men, Zell Ingram in particular, because they were fond of him. However, Frances was disappointed because she believed Rowena shared little with her. Rowena would get ideas for costumes and someone would come in, design them and execute them.

Years later, when the Jelliffes were looking for someone to replace Rowena because she no longer wanted to direct or be in charge of the theater, Frances sent an African American woman to apply for the job of artistic director. According to Frances, the woman, who had a doctorate in theater from Ohio State University, was very well qualified. To Frances's dismay, Rowena told her that the woman was much too qualified for their needs. Instead they hired a man named Benno Frank. This left Frances somewhat bitter, though she and Rowena Jelliffe continued a correspondence for years.

By the time Karamu had acquired new buildings, a theater in the round and a regular proscenium theater, Frances had long since left. She was in New York when she learned that Benno Frank was to speak before a group of theater people at a rooftop restaurant. With her friend, actor Fred O'Neal, they went to hear Frank. Someone asked Benno Frank to speak about his relationship with the Black actors at Karamu. His remarks upset Frances. Characterizing them as demeaning, she threatened to throw him off the roof.

Finally, her appetite to learn more about theater prompted her to go to Connecticut to try to enroll in some of the drama schools there. At one school she visited, the people came up to her and, after looking her over, asked what she wanted. When she told them she was interested in theater and acting, they said, "We're very sorry but we have no scripts that would include you." That incident was repeated at several of the important schools she visited. Rather than dampening her enthusiasm for the theater, it made her more determined.

In 1934, the play that caused her to consider leaving the country was called *Stevedore*, written by Wexler and another man. *Stevedore* was first done on Broadway. When they performed it at Karamu House, it caused a lot of protest because it was critical of the black/white situation, and because of "onstage profanity." (The Plain Dealer) No play before had so vividly portrayed blacks against whites and whites against blacks. In the last scene, Frances stood behind a blockade with a brick in her hand. As she threw it, she said, "I got the god-damned, red-headed son of a bitch." That was her line ending the play.

The authorities first tried to prevent them from opening. The fire department came in and said they had to put in three or four more doors. In the first week, the actors, as well as the Jelliffes, were arrested, held for a few hours and then released.

While *Stevedore* upset many people when they performed

it at Karamu, the first time Frances ever saw a real riot at a theater was at Cleveland Playhouse where she worked a number of times. During one of their performances of *Juno and the Paycock*, written by Sean O'Casey, an angry and determined audience threw rotten eggs and tomatoes. The fact that the audience's rancor was politically rather than racially motivated was of some interest to her. Still frustrated with what she saw as the lack of opportunity to learn more about acting and the theater, she became less satisfied with her life at Karamu. Two other incidents finally convinced her that it was time to move on. The first incident occurred when several fine black actors from New York, among whom was Richard B. Harrison, brought *Green Pastures* to Cleveland. While there, they offered Frances the part of Noah's wife at a very good salary. Excitedly, she rushed to tell Russell and Rowena about the offer. "Oh, Frances," they said. "You can't go. You're a young woman and you really shouldn't go alone." Hoping to discourage her, they gave her three raises in salary within one month. However, nothing they did changed her mind about leaving. The idea of going to Europe was seriously growing in her mind.

Before leaving Karamu, despite having been in eighty-five productions, written and directed some of the plays, made costumes and designed sets - in short, the whole production - she felt she needed to learn more about the technique of theater.

She told her friend, Langston Hughes, about this. He had left Karamu, gone to New York and had become a respected artist, a part of the Harlem Renaissance. He said, "I'll tell you what you should do. The Writer's Congress is coming to New York. At that Congress will be many writers, directors, and people with a great deal of knowledge about theater in the Soviet Union. Plan to be there and meet with someone of importance like Friedrich Wolf. See if he can't direct you where to study theater there." A few years earlier, Hughes had been to the Soviet Union with Louise Patterson and recent graduates from Hampton College to make a film there.

After being turned down so many times, at so many places, early one spring morning, Frances went to New York and to Friedrich

Wolf's hotel. Wolf, who wrote *Sailors of Cattarro* which was being produced by the Theatre Union in New York and several other fine plays, had been living in the Soviet Union for a long time.

In the lobby, she sat down to wait while the desk clerk called up to his room to announce her. After what seemed like a long time, some men came out of the elevator, looked everyone over, and then went back upstairs. This went on for about a half hour. Finally, two of the men came up to her and asked, "Are you the lady who is looking for Friedrich Wolf?"

"Yes, I am. Is it possible for me to see him?" she asked, nervously.

"If you follow me, I'll take you up to him," said one of the men.

As soon as she met Friedrich Wolf, she knew she liked him. They quickly developed an excellent rapport. He spoke English well, and when she told him about the kind of work she had been doing, he brought out pictures of several theaters in the Soviet Union and shots from several of the plays there. She showed him photos she'd brought from Karamu and for over three hours, they sat on the floor and talked. When she rose to leave, he said, "You must come to the Soviet Union. Let me know when you're coming, and I'll see that you're taken care of and set up in a theater." Ironically, when she went there, he was in another country.

Frances left the hotel elated. Before returning to Cleveland, she stopped by Langston Hughes's apartment in New York and told him how successful the meeting had been and that she planned to go to the Soviet Union in the fall of that year.

As a hobby, she collected antique tables and refinished them. For Christmas presents, instead of giving cards or cookies as gifts, she gave tables. When she decided to go to Europe, she sold everything that could be turned into cash - tables, phonographs, radios, everything. Finally, she had enough for a round trip ticket and seventy-one dollars.

On his way to the Coast, Hughes stopped in Cleveland and offered her his bank account in the Soviet Union. He had several books in translation there and had built up a sizeable bank account of rubles. Since he didn't know when he'd be able to go back and use it, he turned the whole thing over to her.

A few weeks before she left, Frances accompanied Russell and Rowena to one of the better schools for workers in Cleveland where she was exposed to Marxism and Leninism. It was also a club where artists exhibited their works. While Russell and Rowena stayed two weeks, she stayed much longer. Shortly thereafter, she packed her bags and set sail for the Soviet Union.

5

FRANCES AND HER MEN

"A little girl and a little boy
in an ecstasy of bliss
said the little boy to the little girl,
'pray, give me just one kiss.'
the girl drew up in great surprise.
"You're a stranger, sir," said she,
but I'll give you just one kiss,
when apples grow on a lilac tree.'

The boy was very sad at heart.
She was the only one
The girl was quite remorseful
at the terrible wrong she'd done
So bright and early the very next morn,
he was quite surprised to see
his little sweetheart standing in the garden
tying apples on a lilac tree."
"When Apples Grow on a Lilac Tree"
(author unknown)

It was late one evening as we sat in her small house in Rosarito, Mexico, that Frances suddenly felt a burst of energy. I was sleepy from the long busy day. I'd driven from Los Angeles to Mexico, spent the afternoon waiting for her to get in the mood to work on her biography, gone out to the town to purchase the evening meal from a roadside stand using my halting Spanish, and then gone to the mercado. Frances tells you exactly what she wants and where to find it. You try to carry out her orders to the letter. We had played Scrabble and as many of her friends know, she usually wins. It was past my bedtime and I was looking forward to sleep on the couch.

Suddenly wide awake, Frances began to talk. I scrambled to find blank tapes on which to record. When those were filled, I recorded over my jazz tapes.

"As a young woman, I had lots of attention from boys. Both P.L and Bill would bring their friends over so that I could teach them to dance. I had plenty of boyfriends, too, all with special interests. One would take me to the opera, another to the theater, and still another would take me to the movies. One man didn't have enough money to take me to all the things I wanted to see because I had such an insatiable appetite; I didn't want to miss anything!

"One young man named Elmer, who later became a professional basketball player, took me to all the athletic things like baseball games and ice skating; he taught me to ice skate. I went out with Billy Banks who sang with Noble Sissle and Jim Europe when they came back from Europe with their first big jazz band and at the Cotton Club.

"Another man everyone called 'Peaches' wanted me to marry him. I'm not sure if he was a gambler or a numbers man. He gambled on luxury steamers that sailed from Lake Erie to Lake Superior and back. Sometimes on the weekends I'd go on these excursion boats with a girl friend. The guys treated us like queens, lavishing us with champagne and food. It was like being in another world.

"A charming man whom I liked very much, Peaches begged my mother and my brothers for my hand in marriage, but I told him I wanted to continue my schooling. He said, 'I don't care what you have to do; I'll pay for whatever. You can do anything you want to. I just want you to be my wife. I'll admit, I won't be home all the time, but we can work out all these things.'

"Zeb Clark, another friend, played saxophone with the Spitoni Brothers who performed at some of the large theaters in the mid west.

When Zeb came out to the west coast to live, we went out a lot together. Like my first husband, George Ferguson, Zeb originally came from Indianapolis. Both were very competitive.

"One time Zeb took me to a matinee at the B. F. Keefe Palace, the loveliest vaudeville theater in Cleveland where Buck and Bubbles, who Zeb knew very well, were playing. They were clever performers and very popular. Just as I started down the aisle, the light man turned the spotlight on me and musicians played, 'Ain't she sweet, see her walking down the street/Now I ask you very confidentially, Ain't she sweet.' I thought, 'Oh, dear, if I live through this.' The verses went on and on until I got to my seat.

"For a while, I went with a man who had a home in Lake Erie, a little town on the other side of Oberlin. Herman was a very good chef, and a thirty-second degree Mason. I knew something about the Masons because my great uncle would recite the rules of the Masons very rapidly and I would have to say them back. I had a very quick mind, and my uncle loved it.

"Herman was very fond of me. The first time I went out with him, he came to Cleveland in a little Ford Roadster, and took me to a party. I had a very nice time. In fact it was mutually enjoyable. The next time he came, we started out to another affair and he said, 'I don't want to embarrass you, but I'm very miserable. I know I can't ask you to help me. If you don't mind, I'll just pull the car over and jerk myself off.' He pulled the car over and went to town.

"Knowing his interest in the Masons, I got him a Mason hat for his birthday. He was so pleased. He took me to some wonderful places in the country to eat. Some were homes turned into restaurants with fireplaces and stairways, immaculate damask tablecloths and candlelight.

"When I told him I was planning to go to Europe, he was very unhappy because he wanted to marry me. 'I have this home with lots of land, near the ocean,' he said one evening. But I wasn't interested in getting married. I was having too much fun.

"One summer vacation, I went to Swarthmore College to study sociology. Rowena had a friend who taught sociology there, and he

39

wrote a glowing letter of reference for me to attend the school. Based on his recommendation, the administration had assigned a large apartment on the third floor for me.

"When I arrived, however, the registration clerk took one look at me, excused herself and went away to consult with someone in the office. When she returned, she said with embarrassment, 'I'm sorry, but we don't have any rooms available.' I was just about to get angry when a young woman who was standing nearby said, 'I'll be happy to share my room with her.' Janet had been born in China. Her parents were missionaries. She had golden hair with a reddish tinge, a tiny waist and shapely legs.

"Thereafter, each summer vacation that I went to Swarthmore to study sociology and anthropology, I roomed with Janet. In the summer of 1932, I met W.E.B. DuBois. He was one of several speakers that day. A handsome man with a goatee, he walked onto the stage and stood behind the podium. The audience grew quiet. He began to speak. 'Racism occurs where you least expect it,' he said and went on to tell the story of his friend, a black man who was the head of YMCA in South Africa. Max had two sons that he wanted to go to school in the U.S. He tried several schools but no one would take them. 'I suggested he send them to a Quaker school in Pennsylvania, but because they were black, they were refused admission...'

"During intermission, I heard mumbling among the crowd. Many were upset; they complained, 'Why should he bring this up?' I went back into the auditorium and saw him sitting alone. I walked over. 'I enjoyed your talk,' I said. 'Would you like to go to town for a beer?' His eyes lit up as he accepted. When the program was over, I drove him to town. We had a beer and a long talk. Little did I know at the time that years later he'd be one of the frequent visitors at my home in California.

"James Weldon Johnson also came to Swarthmore to lecture. James had a light complexion and blue eyes. He wore cream colored suits and a tie that matched his blue eyes. For a while, we went out together. Through Zell Ingram I met writer Claude McKay, a very nice, sensitive man, and a very good cook. I like a well-rounded man. That seems to be one of the requirements for me.

"I knew George Ferguson a number of years before we married. He was a part of the Ann Arbor crowd. Since he was the only one with a car, we would all pile in and go different places. For a long time he wanted me to marry him, but I refused; I didn't want to get married.

"Every week he'd send me a gorgeous present like luggage, a dresser set, silver, perfume, tiny little chocolate candies, or a Longine watch. Before I could send them back, my mother would open them. 'You'd better marry this man,' she'd say.

'But I'm not ready to get married.'

"Then he threatened to kill himself if I didn't marry him. I didn't want him to kill himself, and the social worker in me just knew I could make him the perfect man. Finally, in 1932, I married him. At the time he was living in Detroit. As a wedding present, he gave me my first plane ride from Cleveland to Detroit. After that, we went to N.Y. every six weeks sometimes by plane and sometimes we drove.

"We moved into my apartment over the Settlement House. The apartment had a livingroom, kitchen, and bath. One night, after I had worked all day long, I put the clothes in the bathtub and was bending over it washing them when Fergie came in. 'Oh, I love to see you that way.'

'You love to see me do what?' I said, astonished.

'To see you with your sleeves rolled up leaning over the bathtub washing clothes.'

"He didn't know it, but he'd said the wrong thing. At that moment I decided that was not the kind of marriage I wanted. It was still the first year of our marriage, but I decided then that I was not going to be Mrs. George Ferguson much longer.

"Another incident sealed the fate of our marriage. The year Fergie and I got married, I purchased an automobile for him. One evening I saw him drive by with the car filled with white girls. 'That's the end of the car,' I thought to myself. That was also the end of the marriage. Our divorce became final a year to the date of our wedding. I told the lawyer I didn't want two dates to remember.

"Years later I went back to Cincinnati to visit my brothers, and George, who by that time owned a beautiful hotel in Indianapolis, begged me to come over and spend a weekend at the hotel with him. I went and the damn fool locked me up! In the suite of rooms, roses were everywhere. He'd given orders to the staff not to let me out.

"At that time, the first school in Indianapolis was to be integrated. I begged George to let me watch this momentous event. 'The only way I'll let you go is with me.' We went together but as soon as we returned, I was locked in again. This went on for over three weeks. I tried everything I could think of to get word to my brothers. Then somehow I managed to get a message to Bill. He was there within a day and drove me back to Cincinnati. I thought that was the last I'd see of George.

"Two weeks after I divorced my second husband, Tony Hill, George came out to Los Angeles to ask me to remarry him. He followed me from city to city, wherever I was appearing, with bouquets of long stem roses. Finally, he presented me with a custom-built Jaguar.

"What that Jaguar did for me psychologically was unbelievable. Once I was invited for dinner at a house in the Hollywood hills. I drove up in the Jaguar. At the time I was dabbling in real estate when I heard about a piece of land in Las Vegas which could be used to build a hotel. I thought, if I could raise $375,000, the government would pay the remaining two thirds. So I arranged to have dinner with several millionaires, and I told them about the Las Vegas deal. One of them responded, 'What time can you be in my office tomorrow?' That's what driving a Jaguar did for me.

"My owning a Jaguar was the talk among my friends, as well. Bill and Shirley Taylor, close friends of mine, went back East and were invited by W.E. B. DuBois and his wife, Shirley Graham to dinner. While they were eating, Shirley Taylor said to Dr. DuBois, 'Frances has a Jaguar now.' 'She does?' he said casually.

'Yes, and it's quite beautiful.'

"Later, as they were leaving DuBois suddenly asked, 'How

does she handle it. Is it on a leash? Does she take it for a walk? What does she do with it?' When I heard about the incident, I laughed.

"Finally, I got so sick of George that I told him to take his Jag and go."

6
———

MOSCOW

In the spring of 1934, while the masses of people struggled to survive through the depression years, Frances, with a few lessons in Russian - she had learned to count, to say "hello, goodbye, and where is this and how much is that?" - set out for the USSR.

First she took a plane from Cleveland to New York where she booked passage on the Cunard Line to London. Then she transferred to a Soviet ship which took her across the North Sea. Despite the rough crossing, with the ship tossing from side to side, sending pots off the stove and down the aisle, the Russian crew entertained the passengers; they sang, danced, and encouraged them to join in. Though seasick, Frances was determined to stay up and take in everything.

This was her second time leaving the United States, her first being a car trip across the Midwest and down into Mexico. In September, 1933, shortly after her divorce became final, Frances and Rotha Calhoun, an old school friend, decided to vacation in Mexico. Rotha, who worked as a librarian, wanted to see Mexico, so when she suggested Frances accompany her, Frances leaped at the chance.

In her car, which she had rescued from her marriage to George Ferguson, Frances and Rotha headed west. However, the car broke down in the Ozarks, forcing the two young ladies to stop in a town where just a week earlier, a black man had been lynched. The town folk were just as intrigued with these naive Northern strangers as the young ladies were with them. They were allowed to set up their tarpaulin and sleep on the grounds of a Southern mansion, though warned to "look out for snakes," and in the morning, given a warm send-off.

However, when they reached San Antonio, Texas, for the first time on their trip, they encountered discrimination. At the tourist bureau where they tried to get a visa allowing them to enter Mexico, they were turned away. Undaunted, they drove to the Mexican border. Frances was the first to go before a panel of immigration officers. To her surprise, the Mexican immigration wouldn't allow her in unless she put up $200 which, they said, would be returned upon her departure. When asked what kind of work she did, they stared at her in disbelief when she said she was a social worker and taught theater. All Negroes in the U.S., they assumed, were domestics or menial laborers. Having come that far, she wasn't about to be denied, so she gave them the $200. Interviewed after her, Rotha, who looked Italian and told them she was, paid nothing, which was fortunate because she hadn't brought that much money with her.

Allowed to go on their way, they drove into Monterrey and spent a few weeks there sight-seeing, soaking in the culture, and meeting the people. Leaving Rotha and the car with a family they'd met, Frances took a train to Mexico City. The vacation lasted several weeks, and while it was quite an experience, it did little to prepare her for her two-year European adventure, other than equip her with the knowledge that she could go anywhere and survive.

Among the passengers on the ship heading for the Soviet Union were Anna Louise Strong, journalist, and Willamena Burroughs. A Progressive, Anna Louis Strong organized the first English newspaper in the Soviet Union, the *Moscow Daily News*. When she was expelled from that country, and rejected in the U.S., she settled in China and remained there until her death in 1968.

Willamena Burroughs, a New York schoolteacher, had lost her job when she tried to organize the teachers' union. Ten years later, the union won its case and Burroughs got retroactive pay for those ten years. She was invited to the Soviet Union where she lived for a number of years. Her son Charles and his wife, Margaret Taylor Burroughs, opened the DuSable Museum of African-American

History in Chicago in 1964.

Joining those headed for the Soviet Union where expectations were high, and encouraged by Friedrich Wolfe and Langston Hughes, Frances was eager to see first hand the results of a social and political revolution. In his autobiography, *I Wonder as I Wander,* Langston Hughes wrote that most idealists expected too much of Russia in too short a time. When confronted with the deplorable conditions, the red tape, the purge trials, censorship and arrest, they were greatly disappointed.

On the other hand, Hughes constantly reminded himself and others that, in 1932, when he traveled throughout Russia, the Soviet Union was only fifteen years old. Despite the problems he encountered there, being an American Negro and having experienced prejudice and discrimination in the U.S., he was more forgiving. Caught up in the excitement surrounding the theater movement there, and being a part of the artists' community, Frances encountered few obstacles.

At her hotel, she was given tickets for lunch and dinner. Being a gregarious person, she soon made friends with the young people she met at the New Moscow Hotel, and joined them for dinner and exchanged stories. On the first Sunday she was there, she was invited to attend a big celebration for the Stakhanovites.

One person honored was from the cotton industry. The writers and theater people hosting the party called on her to speak. She gained many friends because of the numerous trade unions and artists represented there.

One of the first places she went was to a travel bureau and, through its manager, she was introduced to others in the city. Because people liked the way she spoke, she found a job right away teaching English at an institute whose pupils were managers of an important industry. In addition to that job, she gave private lessons. One of her students was the wife of Sergei Eisenstat, theatrical and motion picture director.

Adjusting to the cold weather in the Soviet Union was difficult at first. Every day the snow was piled at least ten feet high along the street.   Bundled in a fur-lined coat with a scarf wrapped around her neck and nose, a felt hat that came down over her ears, and rubbers several sizes larger than her feet, Frances trudged around Moscow.

The city fascinated her. She had never seen anything like the crowded tramways filled with people on the top and hanging out the windows, or the subway stations which were used by the various trade unions in competition with each other. Different trade union groups would accept responsibility for the subway entrances.

She describes seeing a Russian woman climb down from a ladder upon which she was working to smoke a cigarette. "This woman who must have been between forty and fifty came down the ladder and as she got to the bottom, she looked up to where she had been working, laying bricks. She took out a packet of cigarettes, hit it, and stuck one in her mouth. She took a match, struck it, and lit her cigarette and I think never in life have I seen anyone earn that smoke more than that woman and how much she enjoyed it! "

Paul Robeson, too, was impressed by what he saw when he visited Moscow for the first time in 1935. He writes:

"The workers are alive. You sense it in the streets, everywhere. You see it in their bearing...In the factories...The theatres and opera houses packed every night by workers. On the trains... men and women studying science and mathematics. In the Soviet Union today, there is not only no racial question; there is not even the concept of a racial question."

Source "Paul Robeson Tells of Soviet Progress," in the Irish Workers' Voice (Dublin) 1935, from RUSSIA AND THE NEGRO, Blacks in Russian History and Thought. Allison Blakely, Wash: Howard University Press. 1986, pg. 149.

* * * * * * * * * * *

In Moscow, housing was very limited. Among other offers, she was surprised when the Levines offered her their apartment. At the time, Irving R. Levine was a foreign correspondent. He and his wife had a very modern apartment with an electric kitchen. It was lovely, but expensive.

Housing was at such a premium that other Americans who had been in the city for much longer than she couldn't understand why she had been offered several places. Two African American school teachers, dissatisfied with conditions in the U.S. and unable to find jobs because of their leftist activity, had moved to the Soviet Union about a year or two before she arrived. Both were from Hampton, Virginia where they had participated in a teachers' strike and had been laid off. Since they had been unable to secure housing, they couldn't understand why she had several offers in the short time she had been there.

Likewise, William Patterson - who Frances dubbed "the fair-haired boy of the Communist Party," because according to Frances, he got first choice of everything - was not too pleased with her coming and getting so much attention. Even he couldn't find an apartment in which to live and had to stay in a hotel.

She would have accepted the Levines' offer for the use of their apartment, but while she was studying at the Meyerhold Theatre, she met Lloyd and Vera Patterson. Both worked at the Meyerhold, he designing sets, she designing costumes and sets. They invited Frances to share their apartment.

About two years earlier, Louise Patterson, who at one time was the head of the School of Business at Hampton College in Virginia, took a group of young black artists and recent college graduates to the Soviet Union to make a film. Among them were Langston Hughes, Henry Moon, Lloyd Patterson, Wayland Rudd, and Ted Posten, one of the first black men to write for the *New York Post*.

Frances had heard that during their stay, several of the group acted like freshmen college kids nearly causing a scandal because of their unrestrained behavior. It was such an embarrassment that she disassociated herself from them.

Feeling that by being with Russian people, she would learn to speak Russian more fluently and learn more about their lives than she could living among Americans, she gratefully accepted the Pattersons' offer. Their apartment consisted of two huge rooms; one served as their bedroom, and the other, they rented out. Frances had one corner and Vera's brother, who was studying for his masters' and learning to fly a gyro plane, had another corner. In another corner there was a man who was studying violin. In the larger of the two rooms, they all ate, worked, and slept. They shared a community kitchen and bath with others in the building.

Several times a week, Frances took classes in Russian, and studied theater. For attending school, she received a stipend from the government, so she was able to purchase most of the things she wanted. Schooling and health care were provided, and housing never took more than ten percent of her salary.

One day, when she was in the apartment alone, two social workers from the trade union came to visit Lloyd Patterson and to see what kind of piano would fit in the space they had. He played piano and sang very well. While the workers were there, Frances showed them some of Vera Patterson's art work. "Lloyd's wife is a great painter, but she has no paper or canvas," she told them. Vera Patterson would tear old peach crates apart, turning them into canvases on which to paint. She'd paint on everything she could find.

Frances hauled out a lot of the paintings Vera had done. When the social worker saw the collection, she said, "This is very good. We shall see that she gets a housekeeper so that she'll have more time available to paint." The idea that a trade union would send social workers to see how they could give you more free time to do your cultural work greatly impressed her.

* * * * * * * * * * *

Both the Russian and the Black men were wonderful to her. Wayland Rudd, who had come over to the Soviet Union with the film group and remained, took her under his wing. An actor with an extraordinary voice, Wayland studied at Meyerhold Theatre and helped her learn Russian.

As an actor, Rudd had appeared in Jasper Deeter's Hedgerow Theatre production of Eugene O'Neill's *Emperor Jones* and had gotten good reviews. Frustrated by racism in the U.S., Rudd settled in the Soviet Union where he studied theatre and appeared in plays around the country.

In an interview entitled "Russia and the American Theatre," The CRISIS, Sept. 1934 pg. 270, Rudd compared theatre in the USSR to theatre in the U.S. At the time Russian theatre was in the experimental stage. Subsidized by the government and under strict censorship, nevertheless, the Russian director worked unhampered by expense limitations. The only thing the government asked is that "plays must be healthful to society." "...[U.S.] they were never interested in society nor plays, nor actors, but in their pocketbooks."

Rudd felt that Negroes in the Soviet Union were treated as equal. "The Negro has long since had something vital to give to theatre but theatre hasn't wanted it, or rather it has only wanted the 'song and dance.' (*RUSSIA AND THE NEGRO*, Blacks in Russian History and Thought. Allison Blakely, Wash: Howard University Press. 1986.)

Though there weren't many, the African Americans she met there didn't want her to go with the Russians, and the Russians said, "When you go home you can go with the blacks." They were always at war with each other. Both had very nice places and she would often go over and cook.

Nevertheless, one problem she had with the Russian men was that they thought they had to make up for all the hurt Blacks had suffered in the states. Consequently, they went overboard in their attempts to shelter her though she didn't want to be sheltered. Or so she thought.

She went on the open road with an American director who had lived for years in the Soviet Union. One of his boyhood friends was a captain in the army, a very handsome young man with dark hair and deep dimples. He had a beautiful wife who had heavy long hair which she pulled over to the side in a coil, and a young son.

The first night they were in Moscow, the head of the touring company had taken a suite of rooms in a luxurious hotel which had been a mansion. He ordered dinner for four of them, the captain and his wife, the tour director, and Frances. There was caviar, turkey, champagne - it was unbelievable. They ate, talked and she was asked to sing.

As the evening progressed, she noticed that the captain would get up from the table and pace the floor. Then he'd come back and sit for a while. After a few minutes he'd repeat those actions. At first she thought it was the custom. Finally she asked her friend, the tour director. He said, "He's a man, and you're a woman. He is very upset about you."

At the end of the evening, the captain's wife said, "Would you come home with us and spend the night with my husband? It would make him so happy and it would make me happy." It took her breath away. "I'm sorry, I can't," she stammered, for she had come from Cleveland where she had been superintendent of Sunday school, had sung in the choir, and she was quite morally upright.

Despite no words of encouragement from her, the captain called her everywhere she happened to be for quite a while. One time when she was eating dinner in the restaurant of a hotel, the waiter approached to say, "You're wanted on the phone." She did her best to avoid him. Looking back on the incident, she felt she was dishonest. Not having the courage to be honest, she never faced it until afterwards. She saw his wife only once after that first meeting, and she met his son. Eventually the captain stopped calling.

****

Frances's primary reason for coming to Moscow was to study theater. In the July 1936 issue of "New Theatre," a magazine devoted to the arts, an ad announced a theater festival in Moscow and Leningrad which was in its fourth successive year.

The Soviet theatre is known for its greatness to theatre lovers and people of the stage in every land. For the fourth successive year, the leaders of the Soviet theatre, opera, ballet and screen have arranged a program of the outstanding productions from their famous repertories. Meyerhold, Stanislavsky, Elanskaya, Natalie Satz, Moskvin, Kachalov!

Group tours were offered to the Soviet Union which included hotels, meals, theater tickets and sightseeing in Moscow and Leningrad for $95 tourist and $165 first class.

Of all the theaters she visited in Moscow, Frances liked Meyerhold Theatre best. Vsevolod Meyerhold, Russian director and actor, who had been sent into exile, had the most modern theater Frances had ever seen.

Another of her favorite theaters was the Tangov where the actors performed plays on a bare stage without anything except costumes. "The actors did everything with their bodies and hands. If the script called for you to be at a table, you would squat as if you were seated at a table. If you were supposed to be eating, you could almost smell the food. If you were playing cards, you could almost see the spade or diamond." Before the theater opened, there was dancing, food, and an orchestra in the lobby. For the children, there was music, puppetry, and materials for them to draw. Between shows someone would tell stories.

In addition to studying at the Meyerhold, she studied at Natalie Satz Children's Theatre. Since working with the children's theater at Karamu, she had always dreamed of forming her own children's theater where the children could learn to dance, sing, and really know how to use their bodies and hands. Years later, when she lived in Mazatlan, she had planned to open a children's theater, but circumstances caused her to abandon the project. At her own place in Los Angeles, she made sure children's theater was always included.

Every Sunday afternoon she and the Pattersons went to the theater. At the Moscow Art Theatre, Frances watched Stanislavski direct Anton Chekhov's *Cherry Orchard* and many of his other plays. Stanislavski created pictures on stage. The actors' movements were always balanced, in harmony, and very formal. Almost everything he did, she wanted to say "Amen." It was like a prayer.

One night at the theater, she was surprised to see her friend John Bovington. A very tall man, about 6'5", John was a great dancer. Frances had known him in Cleveland. Because of his ability to recite poetry dramatically, she would have him read for the children at Karamu. When he'd read Countee Cullen's The *Lost Zoo* , some of the names of the animals were unbelievable to pronounce, but John in his gorgeous voice would read and the children sitting at his feet would be enthralled.

Like numerous other artists, Bovington, it was said, had come to the Soviet Union seeking artistic freedom. When he saw Frances, he turned and walked backwards. "I don't want to take my eyes off you," he said dramatically, opening the door to the auditorium. After letting her pass, he disappeared into the crowd.

* * * * * * * * * * *

One morning Frances awoke with a severe pain in her abdomen. She was rushed to a hospital where she was diagnosed with acute appendicitis. Being a foreigner, before she could be admitted into the hospital, she had to have the proper papers. Of all the people she had to turn to, William Patterson was the only one who was able to cut through the red tape to get her admitted for the operation she desperately needed.

While she lay convalescing in the hospital in Moscow, word of her illness reached her family in Oberlin sending them into a panic. So caught up in the excitement of living in another country, Frances had not written home in six weeks, and her mother Elizabeth was frantic. Her family cabled her and insisted that she come home immediately, but she refused.

This was not the first time they had asked her to come home. Whenever she was broke, she would write to P.L. for money, but he wouldn't send her any until she promised to come home. Many times to survive, she had to pawn her return ticket and redeem it when she had a job.

After two years in the Soviet Union, what finally propelled

her to leave was that her passport expired and rather than go through the enormous amount of red tape to get it renewed there, she made plans to go to Helsinki, Finland. With her funds very low, and Helsinki, the nearest place to get it renewed easily, she said her farewells and boarded a train for Finland.

7

___

HELSINKI AND LONDON

Though she'd lived in the Soviet Union for two years, the few months Frances stayed in Helsinki, Finland in 1935, taught her more about politics than anything she'd experienced before. Upon her arrival, she went to the nearest hotel and booked a room. She spent a few days sightseeing and getting acquainted with the city. At dinner she met some young people who advised her to take the ferry across to Estonia to have her passport renewed because it was cheaper there than in Finland. The following weekend she ferried across to Colleen, Estonia. Intending to stay overnight, she ended up staying there for two weeks at the YWCA.

At the end of the two weeks, she returned to Helsinki and found an apartment right away in a cooperative housing project. Her roommate was a nurse who was away for the summer. A modern building, each apartment was autonomous except for a community kitchen on every floor. On the first two floors were single rooms where foreign dignitaries stayed. Among them were several German Nazi officials.

The Sunday she returned from Estonia, she was down to her last quarter and very hungry. She went out and bought five cents worth of string beans, carrots, potatoes, onions, and a little piece of salt pork and carried them to the community kitchen. As she washed the vegetables, strung the beans, and put them in a pot, she thought, 'That'll keep me for several days until I find out how to earn some money.' No sooner did she get the pot on when the gas meter went out. Broke, hungry, and heartbroken, she walked back to her apartment.

Just as she reached her door, she was called to the telephone. It was a young friend she'd met at a tourist building she visited frequently. There all the music, arts, and crafts were displayed. The young woman whose name was Wuolijoki worked there, and wanting to know as much about the country as possible, Frances had talked with her many times. Wuolijoki invited Frances to meet her friends for dinner at a popular cafe. Without hesitation, Frances accepted her offer. If anything, she'd get a good meal.

At the cafe, Wuolijoki introduced Frances to Ingmar Bergman and other fine writers and artists, many of whom had been political prisoners. It was an enlightening experience, however, one not without consequences. From that day on, Frances discovered she was being followed. Two men trailed her everywhere she went. During the day, it was a tall, thin man in a blue suit, and at night, a stocky man in a gray suit. A carryover from her days in Cleveland, when she'd spend hours hiking through the woods surrounding the city, Frances hiked around the Finnish city, walking the tails off the men following her as they tried to keep up. She almost felt sorry for them.

At the time of Frances's arrival in Finland, relations between Finland and Russia were strained, a remnant of the civil war, and between Finland and Sweden because of the one-time Swedish domination. As a result, the country was bilingual. Even the street signs were written in Finnish and Swedish.

Frances soon became aware of the tension that existed between the two groups; tension that extended into the workplace. If you worked in an office, and an invoice came to you in Swedish and you were Finnish, you would put a stamp on it and send it back and vice versa.

An incident she found humorous at the time occurred when one day, she ran into a very important, wealthy man at whose farm she had visited. He greeted her warmly, for it had been a while since they'd last seen each other. Just before parting, he asked, "How can I reach you? Give me your number and I will call you." Both searched for something on which to write. Finally she found a card. It was blank on one side, but on the other was written the name and address of a former political prisoner. The man looked at the card, his face turning various shades of red, and stuttered, "Don't you have anything else for me to write on?"

Wuolijoki's mother, Frances learned, was Hella Wuolijoki, a famous playwright. Apparently, Wuolijoki had told her mother about Frances because Hella Wuolijoki had chastised her daughter for not introducing her to this fascinating American artist. Hella Wuolijoki invited Frances to her country home in southern Finland. Her home, Marleback, was a favorite meeting place of politicians and literary people like Bertolt Brecht.

The home was surrounded by acres of land, hills, lakes, waterfalls and two nude beaches - one for the men and the other for the women. Frances's room held a big canopied bed and a balcony from which she could view one of the lakes. That day, lolling in the water with the other women present, Frances watched Wuolijoki's mother dictating a play to her secretary, translating it from Finnish to English, pronouncing each phonetic sound, page after page. When lunchtime arrived, the maids brought a large tray and set it on an elevated stone.

In the evening, she dined with ambassadors from several countries, including Germany and Japan, who were frequent guests of Hella Wuolijoki, and listened in shock to talk of territorial expansion. The entire weekend had been quite an education!

The night following her return from the country, the director of a travel bureau called. Frances had been teaching her English. The director offered her a job in the English speaking department of her company.

"If you don't take over this department, Frances," the director said, "I'm going to close it." The English-speaking customers who came for service were rude and discourteous. The director had a big winged chair facing her desk. The last straw came when an American woman came in, sat down in the director's winged chair, put her feet on the arms of the chair, lit a cigarette and blew smoke at the director.

"These Americans are so uncouth, uncultured ugly people," she cried.

Frances accepted the position and landed her best job in Helsinki, the head of the English-speaking department of the travel bureau. Not long after accepting the position, she discovered the director's complaint to be well-founded when a wealthy American woman came into the travel agency. The woman was an ex-patriate who resided in London. She wanted to book a tour of the country and came to the agency to have one set up. However, when she realized that Frances was in charge of the office and that she had to be serviced by her, she became flustered. Frances assured her she would help her to the best of her ability. Barely able to contain her disgust at having to be helped by a black woman, the woman muttered she'd come back.

Frances learned later that among the woman's travel companions was the son of Franz Boaz. As a young girl, Frances had always wanted to study anthropology. On summer vacations from Playhouse Settlement, she took courses in anthropology. For three summers she studied under Franz Boaz and his son, and Melville Jean Herskovitz.

The day after the incident the woman returned, accompanied by Boaz's son. Reluctantly, she apologized. In turn, Frances set up a good tour for her. Their paths crossed again in London when Frances was on her way home. This time, however, the woman sought her out when she learned that Frances was passing through, and gave a party for her.

Being the head of the English-speaking department at the travel bureau had a downside. Most of the college students at the travel bureau wanted the job Frances had and were very upset that she had it. Though she was aware of their jealousy, their disgruntled comments didn't bother her. In spite of it, she was included on their weekend hikes to the countryside. Occasionally, the bureau closed down at noon on Saturday and everyone would go for a hike, sometimes stopping by Sibelius's house for tea with his family.

Other times they'd ride bicycles out to the country to the saunas where they would meet with some of the wives of the employees who had arrived earlier to start the fires and prepare the food. After relaxing in the sauna with the women, Frances would help assemble the meal, eat, and discuss the news of the day.

In addition to working at the travel bureau, she earned money posing for artists. Yet despite her two jobs, her funds were always low. Finally, a friend who worked at another travel bureau invited her to come and live with his sister in Sibbo, just outside of Helsinki. "She gets her housing free with her salary so it won't cost you anything. Besides, she'd love the companionship."

Frances lived at the school in Sibbo for several months, teaching the children English songs and the elders in the town spirituals. Until one day, her friend from the travel bureau called.

"Frances, there's a gentleman here that you might know."

"Why do you think I'd know him?" she asked.

"He's one of your people."

"Hold him until I get there," she shouted. She rushed out, got on the bus and when she got to the travel bureau, there stood this fine looking black man, Harcourt Tines, who was a very important school teacher from New York City. Every summer a group of Negro teachers traveled abroad. The summer of 1936, they happened to be in Helsinki. Tines said he was glad to see her, but not half as glad as Frances was to see him. She hadn't realized how much she missed home until that moment.

It was lunch time and while they were talking, some members of the travel group passed at a distance on their way to the diningroom. To see all those black people in the touring group was thrilling. Tines invited her to join them for lunch, which she did readily, and enchanted them with her Finnish. Coincidentally, among the members of the group was her future husband, Tony Hill. However, at that time, he was little more than a face in the crowd.

* * * * * * * * * * *

After two years of living abroad, she was looking forward to going home. She wired her rich brother P.L. and asked for twenty-five dollars, but it seemed to take forever to get there. During her European adventure, she kept her return ticket. Whenever she needed money, she would pawn it and redeem it when she was solvent again. Finally the money arrived. That and her ticket were all she had to get back to the United States.

Though she was anxious to reach home, Frances decided to stop in London for a few weeks. She visited the theaters, ate in the restaurants, and listened to political speeches in Trafalgar Square. Even though she knew she wouldn't be there long, she enrolled in a four-week course in choral poetry. At the end of the third week, however, she left for home.

On the ship carrying her back to the U.S. were passengers from Ireland and England who deliberately ignored her at first - that is, until she was befriended by the actor Noel Coward. When he asked to sit beside her at the dining table, suddenly she became quite popular. Everyone wanted to know her after that. Every time they played games like shuffleboard and tug 'O war, she was made captain of the team, reminding her of her youthful days in Cleveland when everyone wanted to be on her team. When she got home, she laughed at their snobbery and ugliness.

As the ship slowly crossed the ocean, bringing her closer and closer to the country of her birth, a thought kept running through her mind. She knew she could never give up the theater, but after studying in the Soviet Union, she thought, "How in the hell am I going to go back to the states and play Aunt Jemima roles?"

8

YOU CAN'T TAKE IT WITH YOU

The depression that had gripped the nation had not lessened by the time Frances returned from Europe. Upon her arrival, she went straight to Cleveland where she discovered her brother Bill had rented an apartment and furnished it so that the two of them could share it. She had no thought of staying in Cleveland, but was at a loss as to how to explain to her brother that she needed a change. They had always been close and she didn't want to hurt him.

For two weeks, she was in turmoil trying to find a way to tell Bill that she didn't want to live in the city of her younger days. Finally she told him. Things were happening in New York and she just had to be there.

She describes her return in her notebook.

"I remember when I returned from having lived and studied in Europe for 2 years - I had worked at the Settlement in Cleveland and the directors had made me promise to come back to work there when I returned. But after learning all the things that I learned - going through the little minds and the red tape of organized Settlement thinking was not anything I looked forward to doing. I had not discussed this with my family. When I arrived in Cleveland my young brother who had lived with me in an apartment at the Settlement before I left for Europe had gone into hock to furnish a new apartment with store-bought furniture for me and him to live - I had been an avid antique collector [and] before I left had to rent a big garage to house the beautiful tables and things that I'd found - I had a wonderful old carpenter who fixed them up, refinished them and I'd give them away to friends for birthday or Christmas presents. Here I am enclosed in ickying newly purchased - overpriced   furniture my little brother thought we could share the costs - At this time my brother delivered special delivery letters for a living. So it became my troublesome duty to tell not only the people at the Settlement who had by the way hired 5 people to replace me on my return [and] had honored me with a tremendous welcome home party. Now I must inform them that I could not continue to work there - But added to this, I must face my young brother whom I loved almost as much as life itself, that I was leaving in 3 days to live permanently in NYC..." Her decision caused a strain in their relations that lasted years.

Frances went to New York with the intention of going into business with Dick Huey, a very fine actor, who played many roles on Broadway, most recently in the cast of *Porgy and Bess*. "A good-looking dark-skinned beautiful man, Dick knew the King's English and literature very well." Huey had taken over the basement of a building on 135th St. and Lenox Ave. very near the YMCA where Paul Robeson started, and had opened a barbeque restaurant which he called "Aunt Dinah's Kitchen." At night he used the restaurant for a theater.

Putting what little money she had into the business, Frances settled down for her new life in the city. However, less than two weeks later, she received a call to audition for a play on Broadway. Having spent two years studying theater in Europe, she was determined that if they asked her to do dialect to please some foolish people, she would refuse.

The play for which she auditioned was *You Can't Take it With You*, and to her delight, her lines were not written in dialect nor did she have to wear a kerchief. The first line she had as she came on stage was, "Goddam those flies in the kitchen!"

Written by George S. Kaufman and Moss Hart, it was a good comedy with a supportive cast that included Ham Tree Harrington in a role originally written for Oscar Polk, a black actor, who looked very much like Stepin Fetchit. Among theatre people, Polk was known as Kaufman's rabbit's foot because every play Kaufman wrote was successful when he included a part for Polk.

However, by the time Frances joined the production, Polk had left. Assuming his role was a comedian named Ham Tree Harrington whom she got to know very well during the run of the play.

"Ham Tree was married to a beautiful Italian woman who loved him very much. She took good care of him. One night, Ham Tree went out. Before he left, she asked him what he'd like for dinner. 'I'd like some spaghetti with lots of meat in it and some cold lemonade,' he said. Ham Tree's wife worked all day getting this meal together.

"At dinnertime, Ham Tree didn't arrive. Eight o'clock, he still hadn't arrived. Nine o'clock, ten o'clock, no Ham Tree. Then around midnight, in walks Ham Tree bleary-eyed and kind of high, barely able to function. He takes off his clothes and gets into bed. His wife is so mad, she goes into the kitchen, picks up this whole pot of spaghetti. 'You ordered this, and here it is.' She dumps the whole pot of spaghetti on his head. 'And there's something else you asked for.' She pours a pitcher of lemonade on him. When he told me that story, I fell out laughing."

Shortly after Frances joined the cast, *You Can't Take it With You* went on a lengthy road tour. The first stop was in Chicago where it ran for two years. She found an apartment at Lincoln Center, an entire building devoted to housing notable artists, writers and other progressive women who came to town. Among the residents were Louise Patterson, who later married William Patterson, and writer/journalist Thyra Edwards.

Frances shared an apartment with Lillian Sommers, a tall, attractive black woman from Boston. Sommers was the head of all the black social workers. Having been a social worker at the Settlement, Frances found she and Sommers had much in common and they got along well. Sommers had exquisite taste. She had furnished her lovely apartment with Persian rugs and delicate crystal.

During the week, the Center served breakfast and dinner in their diningroom; however, on the weekends, because the Center was closed, the ladies kept food in their apartment refrigerator. Each week they would take turns buying food, flowers and liquor with which to entertain their many guests.

Despite the Depression, having steady employment in the theater and living at the Center afforded Frances with luxuries available to few. In the 1930's there were several Negro dress designers living in Chicago. Frances had suits especially made for her with skirt-length coats to match, and matching hats.

Twice a day, Frances and Sommers would go horsebackriding very early in the morning, then again in the afternoon before Frances went to work, except on Saturdays because she had both a matinee and an evening performance. On Sunday mornings, they would start out at five o'clock and ride for one or two hours.

"A very good horse woman, Lillian had her own horse. I rented one by the month. One bridle path ran through the main districts in Chicago, and another ran along the beach where we usually went. After riding, we would stop for coffee and fruit juice, and finally a massage. A massage after horsebackriding, leaves you feeling sorry for everyone else in the world.

"Following the massage, we'd take a nap, and when we woke up, we would have lunch. At four o'clock, anyone of importance in town came to our apartment for cocktails. On Sunday afternoons, all the best available men lined up to see us. One of them was A. Phillip Randolph. I had met him at Karamu when he came to speak at the fathers' club. His work as a trade unionist took him all over the country so that whenever we were working in the same city, he always came to see me.

"Another resident at Lincoln Center was a tall, thin rather attractive, but gawky English woman, a social worker. One morning she asked me if she could go horsebackriding with me. I said yes and we went to the stable. Except for the horse I rode every week, all the good horses had been taken. The only other horse available was a big old lanky horse that hadn't been put out in the field to run for a long time.

"I climbed on my horse and waited for my friend to mount hers. I noticed that she was having trouble getting on her horse, so I got off mine to help her get her feet in the strap. Once she was settled, I went over to my horse, put one foot in the stirrup and as I swung the other leg over, I accidentally kicked the horse. He started running lickity split through the traffic with me dangling, struggling to hold on, one leg up in the air. Finally, the horse threw me off, its left hind hoof kicked me and broke my jaw in three pieces.

"As I lay on the pavement, bleeding like a stuck pig, a crowd gathered around me. I heard someone say, 'Oh my God. He's kicked all her teeth out.' 'Not all,' I wanted to say. Two of the teeth that were broken were on my dentures. But because I had to hold my mouth together, I couldn't say anything. Finally, I was taken to a lovely little hospital owned by a group of black doctors.

"When Lillian heard about it, she came rushing over with a bottle of very good cognac. 'Now, now, Frances. Don't you worry. Everything's going to be alright.' It wasn't long before all the distinguished doctors at the hospital came to visit me. Throughout my brief stay, I never had an empty room.

"With my jaw wired together, I had to learn a new speech pattern. I couldn't go back to work immediately; however, after a couple of weeks, I went on stage with my jaw wired and threw my lines so the audience could understand them.

"During my stay in Chicago, my mother Elizabeth came to live with me for a while. One Sunday Mother decided she wanted to go to a luncheon at an Episcopal church she was attending. I had to be at a rehearsal so I dropped her off at the church and gave her money for a cab home. A few hours later, when I came back from the theater I was surprised that Mother hadn't returned. I looked everywhere but couldn't find her. It was one of the few times in my life that I was scared shitless. My mother lost in Chicago! and I'd left her alone. My brothers would kill me!

"After lunch, Mother, who was such a primadonna, had gotten into a cab and was just bubbling over with stories about her daughter who was in the theater and all the things mothers talk about. She was a jolly person and a great teller of tales. People liked being around her.

"After listening attentively for several minutes, the cab driver asked, 'Madam, where do you want to go?' She said, 'Why bless you honey, I don't know. It's a hotel. I don't know what street it's on, and I can't think of the name.' Then she remembered it had a canopy that went out to the curb. Through her description of the building and the diningroom, the driver knew it as one of the newest hotels for Blacks. After that incident, I sat up all night long sewing tags with her name and address in every garment she wore.

"Because of the parties I attended, I got to know quite a few men some of whom thought they could get to me through my mother. They spoiled her, bringing her boxes of chocolates and because they knew she loved strawberries, even though at that time of year, they were out of season, they saw to it that Mother got strawberries anytime she wanted.

"One evening, a group of social workers some of whom I'd met when they were touring in Finland had a party and I was invited. The room was fairly crowded by the time I arrived. I was engaged in a conversation with some people, when I happened to glance up to see a charming man enter the room with another social worker. As the evening wore on, I felt his eyes on me wherever I went. Then, I heard him say to the woman with him, 'Wait a minute. Watch her. Isn't she the most interesting woman you have ever seen?' Finally we were introduced.

"Like most of the people at the party, William Anthony Hill, too, was a social worker. A brilliant man with exquisite taste, a photographic memory, Tony had a great deal of tenacity and determination to accomplish whatever he wanted to do.

"He lived in an apartment that was so unique, whenever the tour busses went through Chicago, they would point out his apartment and announce- 'Mr. William Anthony Hill's apartment.'

"Tony had such superb taste that whenever any of the guys in his crowd wanted to buy a suit, shoes, raincoat, they never bought it unless Tony approved of it. When I'd known him barely a week, we were sitting in his livingroom with a group of his friends. He turned to me and said, 'I went downtown and I saw a blazer. I want you to take a look at it and tell me if I should get it.' The guys were stunned because here was the master of fashion asking my opinion of what he should wear.

"He introduced me to many of his friends, some of whom were a part of the Renaissance crowd who had moved to Chicago. One good friend was Fletcher Butler, a virtuoso on the piano who played for wealthy people like the Cunninghams who would fly him all over the United States. In his house, which he shared with his father who lived downstairs, Fletcher had a baby grand piano which he played at the many parties he hosted.

"Both Tony and my mother competed for my attention. When they both got sick at the same time, I was pulled in two directions. Finally I got a nurse for my mother, but every other minute Tony would call me. Every day he'd call and say, 'Look, I need you. Lizzie has a nurse. Get over here!' I have a very acute ear for speech. Though Tony stammered, I was never bothered by it."

From their first meeting Frances and Tony were inseparable. However, after two years in Chicago, the casts received word that the play was moving across country.

* * * * * * * * * * *

ON TOUR

During the 1930's, touring with a mixed company called for a certain amount of juggling on the part of the production managers and flexibility on the part of the cast. In some towns, because of racial segregation laws, they couldn't all stay together. The white actors stayed at a hotel while the black actors had to stay with black families who would rent them rooms. In other towns, whenever possible, the company would take over a section of a rooming house so that they could all stay together.

Whenever they would go into a small town for a one-night performance, their routine seldom varied. After booking rooms for the night, and organizing their costumes, and before rushing to the theater, they would purchase food items such as steak sandwiches, pie and coffee from the local restaurant and quickly eat them in their rooms. Rarely did they have time to sit down to eat together.

One night, after a performance, several of the cast members found they were hungry again. This time rather then pick up food to eat in their rooms, some of them decided to find a restaurant, sit down and have a full meal. While the other black members of the cast returned to their rooms, eager for a hot cooked meal, Frances went along with those in search of a comfortable place to eat. They found a nice restaurant, and being the only black member of the cast, Frances, who was always prepared for possible rejection, told them, 'You all sit on the stools along the bar and I'll sit at the end.'

Their waiter, a boy of seventeen, took their orders. After a short while, he returned with their food. Right in the middle of serving them, his boss called him over and whispered in his ear. He came back and said to Frances, "I'm sorry, Ma'am. My boss says I can't serve you."

Ignoring him, she kept talking and eating. The boy repeated what he'd said.

"I heard you," she said, fairly annoyed, but determined to finish her meal. The boss came over.

"Look, Lady," he said. "If I serve you, they'll put me in jail."

"What do you want us to do. We have our food," she responded.

He looked at all the steaks on the counter and then at them. "Well," he said, glancing around the almost empty room, "if you all will move over here," he indicated a large round table in the corner, you can finish your meal."

After a while, the boy came over and started a conversation with her. "You know, my brother plays football."

"Good," she said.

"Wouldn't you like to see a picture of my brother?" He stayed beside her until everyone finished and prepared to leave. She knew it was his way of apologizing, but it didn't lessen the pain.

Frances encountered incidents similar to this many times in

her travels. "I was going to Chicago from Los Angeles and we had difficulty with the fog. The plane couldn't continue its flight so we had to land in Amarillo, Texas. The stewardess said they hadn't expected to stop therefore, they didn't have food on the plane. There was a little restaurant near the airport, she said, and we could have breakfast there.

"All the passengers and crew went in to this little restaurant in Amarillo and some of us sat down at a U-shaped counter. The waitress looked at me and said, 'I'm sorry, I can't serve you here, but if you'll go into the room in the back, I'll see that you get your order.' I just sat there, numb. I took out a cigarette and lit it. The waitress came back over and said, 'I told you to go in the back.' I looked up at her and said, 'You told me, but I didn't tell you where you could go. My grandfather lost four sons in World War I fighting for democracy. This doesn't make any sense to me.'

"At the other end of the counter were the stewardess and the captain who were getting their breakfast served. I went over to them. Though I didn't know a damn thing about interstate laws, I said, 'You people have gotten yourselves into an awful fix. You'll have a big lawsuit because you've brought passengers in here and they can't be served.' The stewardess sympathized with me. She said, 'I know exactly how you feel. If you go into the back, I'll go with you.' 'Evidently you don't understand because I'm not going anywhere,' I said.

"At that moment the waitress came with a plate of eggs, pancakes and sausages and set them down before the stewardess. 'This just happens to be what I was going to order,' I said. 'I'll take this. You can sit where I was.' I sat down and ate my breakfast. When I finished, the man on my left glanced over and said, 'I'm from Canada. May I order you another cup of coffee?'

"When I got back on the plane, what had happened had gotten around to all the passengers. I could feel the tension. Half the people were glad I'd stood up and fought, and the other half probably wanted to strangle me.

"One had come to expect that sort of treatment in the South,

71

but to a degree, the North was almost the same. We were playing in Chicago and Hilda, an actress, would pick up a sandwich from a restaurant whenever she played matinee and take it to her room as I did. She told me about the time matinee was cancelled and she decided that instead of bringing a sandwich to her room, she'd eat at the restaurant. The waitress refused to serve her. 'The others don't want to eat with you,' the waitress said. Hilda leaned over the counter and yelled, 'Any of you all don't want to eat with me?' She got served because of the protest of the other patrons. When she got ready to pay for her meal, she handed the waitress a two-dollar bill saying, 'Here, this is for you and your education because you need it.'

The members of the cast of *You Can't Take it With You* were wonderful to work with. One in particular, Patty, who was cast as a ballet dancer, and Frances, grew quite close. Through Patty, Frances met Gene Kelly and others she would later work with in New York and Hollywood.

Out of all the cast members, Patty told Frances that she was the only one she felt she could talk to. She confided that during her graduate year, she'd taken drugs to get through all the tests and had gotten hooked. It never interfered with her performance, but there were always anxious moments wondering whether she'd make it to the theater on time. Though Frances was concerned with Patty's welfare, urging the young woman to seek help, Patty assured her that she could handle it.

In Cleveland, Frances's sister-in-law Cora invited the entire company to her home for pigs' feet, collard greens, and corn bread. When they were ready to leave for Detroit, their next scheduled stop, Patty was not at the station. Frances's brother Bill went to look for her and found her in her hotel room, completely out of it. All her clothes were soaking in the bathtub. He wrung out the clothes, got her together and drove her to Detroit in time for their next performance. Patty's drug use continued to destroy her. Many times she would get into a taxi and not know where she was going.

The company moved on to Milwaukee where Frances met the head of the Sociology Department at a University in Milwaukee.

His wife, a musician, invited her to their house for Sunday dinner. With her permission, Frances took several of the members of the cast along. It was a lovely evening during which her host demonstrated a technique she'd developed for playing music using charts with chords which she had transposed into numbers. Before dinner she gave each of them an instrument and using the charts she provided, they played a concert in what Frances termed as "amazing harmony."

When *You Can't Take it With You* performed in Dallas, Texas, Frances decided on her day off to visit a department store she'd heard a lot about. "I had heard about Neiman-Marcus and what wonderful and exotic things they had to sell. I thought I shouldn't leave Dallas until I buy something from them. I asked the driver of the bus what street I had to get off. He said, 'Oh, it's just about two or three blocks.' I sat down behind him and he kept driving. Then suddenly, he looked back and saw me there. 'Woman, you don't sit there!' I said, 'You said I only have a couple of blocks to go and I thought I'd sit here so I'd be sure to get off at the right place.'

'I don't care, lady,' he said emphatically. 'You can't sit here.'

'Then I'll just stand here for the next couple of blocks. I always forget I'm in the United States,' I said."

9

___

RENASCENCE

A fter the tour of *You Can't Take it With You* ended, Frances moved back to New York and for a while stayed with her friend Garnet at 312 Manhattan Avenue. She got a job as an interviewer for an employment agency in Brooklyn. Her work day began at 6:30 a.m. and ended late in the afternoon. In the evenings, she worked as wardrobe mistress in a theater on Broadway. Liz Rosenthal, who once taught at Karamu House in Cleveland and whom she had met again while on tour, got Frances the job working with her and Jerome Robbins on an all-black musical production. They worked together all summer. What Frances learned about lights from Rosenthal, she was later able to use at Actors' Lab in Hollywood.

In the 1930's, like theaters across the country, theaters in New York were segregated. Members of Actors' Equity refused to play in those theaters. Because Frances was an active member of the union, some of the members came to her and asked if she would help organize a big protest march against the segregated theaters. They wanted a prominent name out front, so they asked her to contact Adam Clayton Powell. Though she had never met him before, she went to see him. This tall, handsome man greeted her warmly, listened to her appeal and when she'd finished, enthusiastically consented.

In addition to being active with Actors' Equity, Frances became involved with the newly formed Negro Actors' Guild. The United Actors' Guild of America had allocated a stipend to be used by its members to develop projects; however, few members applied for it. Then Noble Sissle and Leigh Whipper decided to organize a Guild and apply for the money. They formed the Negro Actors' Guild which included Bill Robinson, Louis Armstrong, Ethel Waters, Marian Anderson, J. Rosamond Johnson, Georgia Burk, and Evelyn Ellis, and Rev. Adam Clayton Powell, Jr. among others. Frances had met many of them when they had visited Karamu House.

The function of the Guild was mostly social, to provide for fellow actors who were out of work or hospitalized. According to Frances, Noble Sissle, Freddy Washington, James Weldon Johnson, and Paul Robeson were the most active in keeping the guild going.

Noble Sissle was the first president, Freddy Washington, the executive director, and Edna Thomas, the executive secretary. When Washington went on the road with *The Member of the Wedding,* Edna Thomas replaced her as director. Leigh Whipper told Frances about the Negro Actors' Guild, and she joined and became one of the founding members.

* * * * * * * * * * * *

"While I was on the road with *You Can't Take it With You,* Tony wrote that he'd decided to change jobs and was going to Albany, New York for an interview. Coincidentally, the person who interviewed him was a friend of mine, a social worker from Cleveland. Once Tony got the job, I would go up to visit him there and we would sail down the Hudson River together.

"One day he called me and said, 'I've had my blood test. Have you had yours yet?' Dr. Maynard, a doctor friend of mine, gave me a blood test. Everyday, I would pester the doctor to give me the results and he would tease me. Finally, he gave me the okay and I rushed up to Albany to Tony. After writing our own special vows, we had a simple wedding ceremony that surprisingly was announced in one newspaper in Albany. The headline read 'Social Worker marries prominent artist.'

"We spent our wedding night in Tony's apartment located on

the top floor of an old brick building with a thirty-foot high ceiling. Sometime during the night, we were suddenly awakened by a great commotion. There, flying around the ceiling were bats! I was terrified. Tony spent the rest of the night chasing them.

"As we sailed down the Hudson River to New York, Tony said, 'I want you to keep your name and your own entity(sic).' For years, on our anniversary, I'd present Tony a copy of our vows.

"To celebrate our wedding in New York, we invited several friends to brunch at a club we knew downtown. My cousins Charlie and Oscar Hunter, Garnet and Zell Ingram, Tony's friends which included writer Harold Jackman and his sister, came, and after eating a delicious meal, we danced the afternoon away. Among the wedding gifts we received were Gorham Silver and Havelin China.

"Until he was able to transfer to the city, Tony stayed in Albany while I searched for an apartment for us to live. At one place, the landlord said she wouldn't mind renting to me, but the neighbors didn't want me. So I visited every apartment in the building and finding no one who objected, I went back to the landlord and told her what they said. Reluctantly, she agreed to let me rent the apartment, but by then I didn't want to live there.

"That same day, I found another place, on 102nd St. and Third Ave., a little two story brick house with a charming yard. The owners lived next door. When I went in, the owner, an Italian woman, said she'd already accepted a down payment on the house. 'Let me stay and visit with you a while,' I said. She hesitated. I followed her into the kitchen. 'I'm a bit busy,' she said as she plunged her hands into a sink filled with soapy water and dirty dishes. I took off my coat and told her I would help her. We worked the rest of the day doing laundry, dusting and straightening up her apartment. By late afternoon, just as I was about to leave, she said, 'Any time you want the apartment, it's yours.'

"The apartment was located in a predominantly Italian neighborhood. In the space behind a group of buildings was a large garden of fig trees. Many of the neighbors made wine out of the figs and every once in a while, they would give me a gallon. It wasn't long before I knew many of the neighbors as well as the merchants.

"The block along Second Avenue and First Street was lined with pushcarts filled with everything imaginable, - costumes for the theater, lampshades, everything. A few blocks from Park Avenue, beneath the el trains were shops where you could get everything from food to furniture. I shopped there for material which I would take downtown to use to design sets and make costumes.

"Nearby, the shopkeepers had purchased four unit apartments which they used for storage. I became so well-known among them, sometimes they would give me the key to the places where they kept their stock. One woman vendor told me she wanted me to have her shop after she died. I was touched that she thought so well of me. A good friend, Bill Bailes and I collaborated on a book about New York markets where you could buy anything from stoves to plumage.

"Knowing the workings of the government, it wasn't long before Tony was transferred to the New York State Dept. of Social Welfare to do public and relief assistance. Alfred Eisentat worked there as well, and sometimes he and his wife would come to lunch with us.

"Tony was such a tightwad, he'd give me fifteen cents to go to the market. 'Take this,' he would say. 'I know you'll come back with $100 worth of goods.' And I would. I'd bring back partially finished hats, bolts of cloth. I could go into a ten cents store and come out looking like a million dollars.

"After a year, Tony and I moved to 103rd Street into a lovely six-room apartment. The building was three stories tall, and because we lived on the top floor, we made a garden on the roof.

"Life with Tony was never dull. For one thing, he was the messiest man I'd ever known. Tony never picked up after himself. He'd come in and drop whatever he was wearing wherever he happened to stop. In the bathroom, he'd leave the tops off the toothpaste, and every jar and bottle he used. It was extremely annoying. Finally I decided I wouldn't pick up after him any more. After all, I worked as he did, shopped for food, and prepared meals.

Still, no matter what I would say, I couldn't break him of the habit.

"Then one day when I came in from work, I went from room to room drawing pictures of each room showing where he'd dropped his clothes. Next I tacked the pictures all over the apartment. Then I picked up all his clothes and took them into the livingroom. I hung a sock on the chandelier, his pants I threw over the lampshade, a shirt I draped over the sofa. When I finished, the place looked ridiculously funny.

"A short time later, Tony came home. He looked at the drawings, and at the clothes all over the place, and was so embarrassed that his friends would discover what a messy person he was. I told him, 'I will take care of the kitchen and the bedroom, but you'll have to take care of the rest of the apartment, and you can't hire anyone to help you.'

"Tony never did anything in a small way. After that incident, he enrolled in the Pratt Art School and took up interior decorating. He went out and brought all new furniture in thick bamboo and glass top tables. He filled the apartment with an assortment of plants, and the piece de resistance - a full size baby grand that took up a whole room. He was having so much fun, I got jealous.

"As a member of Actors' Equity, I could get the best tickets to concerts, and operas for only 50 cents. And every week we gave parties inviting people who were currently appearing at Carnegie Hall, and friends he'd met at the Pratt Art School and at Carnegie Tech.

"I had kept in touch with my friend Patty who had settled in New York, and she introduced me to Bill Bailes, a charming man quite tall, with thick curly hair. Bill had studied at the Gutrie School in Minnesota and went on to teach ballet at a school in Vermont one half of the year and the other half, he danced with a dance company.

"Patty also introduced me to actor and dancer Gene Kelly and his wife, and Jim Beard, the gourmet chef. Jim, who was from Seattle, would come over and teach me to make cakes without using baking powder and other exotic dishes. He lived on Third and 102nd Street. Whenever it was strawberry season, Jim would telephone and say, 'Call all your friends.' Then he would come over and make jam.

MEET IT, GREET IT, AND DEFEAT IT

"Another woman I met through Patty was Cecil Kitkat. A friend of Bill Bailes, Cecil lived with us for over a year. Cecil was a dance teacher who taught Delacroix Erhythmics and played several instruments including the recorder and the virginal piano. Cecil had frizzy hair, and long thin legs and seemed to be all arms and elbows. She was from England, but having lived all over the world, had developed a bastard speech. She loved to make fresh marmalades, jams, and jelly. Every night we'd sit down to dinner which included the jellies she made. Through the influence of Cecil and Bill Bailes, I got the opportunity to lecture at Carnegie Tech.

"I met Ves and Nice Harper, a young couple who lived near us. Nice, who was part Portuguese and part black, worked as a model. Tall and slender, Nice was exotic looking with big gray eyes, and gorgeous brown skin. Her husband, Ves, a great gourmet cook, worked in theater. Ves designed all his wife's clothes. If she had a gray fur cape, she'd have a matching gray vest, skirt and ha r cast members searched for places to stay, Ves and Nice invited me to stay with them. When Alvin Ailey was getting started, I introduced him to Ves Harper and Ves became stage manager, costume designer, and did all the technical work for his productions. They went on a tour of the Orient. After settling in Denmark, Ves became the wardrobe designer for the Royal Ballet in Copenhagen.

"Tony was a snob. He always thought he knew everything. To teach him a lesson, I would invite graduate students from Columbia to spend the weekend. Because they were more knowledgeable about their field than he was, Tony would have to sit back and listen. Occasionally, a student from Julliard School of Music would stay the weekend. Then, whenever we gave a party, ten or fifteen of our guests would contribute $50.00 each towards a stipend for six students, and in return, once a month students from the school would give concerts for our guests.

"New York was brimming with wonderfully interesting people. A good friend of Tony's, pianist, composer Margaret Bonds moved from Chicago to New York. I found her an apartment on 101st Street. Though she was married and had a little girl, Margaret was madly in

80

love with Langston Hughes. She practically worshipped him as did many other females I knew. Through Margaret, I met Leontyne Price, Roland Hayes, and many others she composed for. In the 1950's, she had more music registered with ASCAP than any other female.

"One day, someone told us that Jacob Lawrence was living in a loft on 125th Street and Seventh Avenue near the el trains. Tony and I went up to see him. He was in the process of creating the 'Migration' series and sixty canvases lined the walls of this huge room. While we watched him work, he'd dab a touch of yellow, green, or blue paint on each of the canvases in turn giving them a harmony of color; it was truly amazing.

"Finally, I said, 'Jake, where do you sleep?' 'Anywhere I can find room.' 'Where do you eat?' I saw no table and not much of a kitchen. He shrugged. I told him where we lived and said, 'If you ever want some collard greens and corn bread, come on over.' The next weekend, he came over for dinner. After that, our friendship grew, and consequently, when Tony and I came to Los Angeles, the first of two major art exhibits we put together featured Jake's 'Migration' series.

"Geraldine Desmond, who for years wrote the society column for Jet Magazine, had a penthouse apartment downtown where she threw lavish parties. She kept not less than $1000 worth of liquor in her bar. At her house, I met Alberta Hunter. Some weekends we were invited to Madam C. J. Walker's estate to parties hosted by her daughter, A'Lelia Walker. These were excellent parties.

"Through my friend Garnet, I got to know Ethel Waters who lived diagonally across from her, and Ralph Ellison who lived in the same apartment building. Garnet let me help her organize the woman's auxiliary of the Urban League. Among its members were prominent New Yorkers like Mollie Moon. Once a year, the auxiliary gave a fancy costume ball which we attended.

"Life was full. I was working several jobs while Tony went back to school to get his master's. I don't know how I did it. During one summer, I made two films with Oscar Micheaux, *Lying Lips*

(1939) and *The Notorious Elinor Lee* (1940).

    "Years later when I had been living in Los Angeles for a while, Tony's brother, Henry, came out to visit. I wanted him to see one of these famous houses on the hill. Ben, the comedian, who had a house there was out of town but he allowed us to tour his house. When we got there, a friend of Ben's greeted everyone in our party warmly except me. He looked at me with such a scowl, I thought, 'I've never met this man before. Why is he frowning at me?'

    "He showed us the first floor and the second floor. It was mighty fancy. On our way out, we stopped in the lobby. He looked so sullen and hostile that finally I said, 'Pardon me, I haven't done anything to you. I don't remember having met you before.'

    'Do anything to me!' he said. 'You were the mother in that *Lying Lips* and you treated that sweet little girl awful. I'll never forgive you.' All I could do was laugh.

    "I was named chairperson of the activities committee of the Performing Arts Center, a part of the YMCA at 58th and Broadway. One of my duties included helping young art groups prepare for their performances. Many of the boys and girls whose parents were artists were enrolled.

    "The Children's Aid Society built a huge gorgeous center in Harlem for children and young people. Because I was on the executive board of the Performing Arts Center, and because I knew how to get around red tape having worked at Playhouse Settlement in Cleveland, they asked me to run the Center's drama department.

    "Mr. Gregory, the man in charge of the Center, looked very much like Muhammed Ali, except unlike Ali, he didn't have a mind of his own. He did whatever he was told to do. From the outset, he was ready to criticize whatever I tried to do.

    "One of the first things I did was to go downtown and find out who was on the board of the various projects the Society had already set up. I found the names of many prominent actors and other artists and immediately contacted them and asked if they'd be on my board at the Harlem Community Arts Center. This gave us such prestige that any idea the children or I came up with, no matter how controversial, we were able to get it done. If there was a question I'd simply say, 'What do you want me to do? Go back and tell the board?' I got many things done that way. Mr Gregory was awed. He didn't know how to criticize anything I did because I had these people behind me.

"The Children's Aid Society had a camp that was supposed to be the last word in camps. No Blacks had ever gone to it. I told my board I wanted to take some children from Harlem there and they set about getting it for me. I gathered together the best writers, musicians, composers and dancers, and took them along with the kids from different centers in the city, Polish, African Americans, Irish, and Asian to the camp for two weeks.

"We set up discussion groups so that the participants could learn more about each other's culture. The youngsters discovered how much they had in common. For example, the Irish youngsters told us about the situation in Ireland that was so bad, in order for teachers to teach the children, they had to go into the bush. It was an eye opener for all but, especially for the black youngsters who didn't know that the Irish had this type of problem to deal with. We found out what good friends we could be by cutting through and learning about each other.

"From this project, we wrote a play set in the interior of the Statue of Liberty and invited others from centers around the city. An exciting production, it was the first time this was ever done in New York.

"In the midst of all this activity, I discovered I was pregnant. When I told Tony, he said it was a dreadful world to bring a black child into. Besides, being the eldest in his family, and having to rear his younger siblings, he didn't want to raise any one else.

"The smells of the neighborhood that had always enticed me, now made me sick. Now the pungent odor of garlic made me throw up. For weeks I hoped Tony would change his mind; however, he was adamant. 'No more changing diapers.'

"Finally, I went to my doctor, Dr. Maynard who lived across the street from Garnet. When he examined me, he discovered I had a fibroid tumor. I went in for an operation where he removed not only the tumor, but also the baby and everything else.

"In 1939, the week of the Juneteenth celebration was black week at the New York World's Fair. The organizers wanted to have a performance by black dancers; however, they didn't know of any Negro dance groups. They called me and I contacted a group of modern dancers I knew from Karamu.

"Shortly before we left New York, as a part of the Writers' Project, I worked with the National Youth Authority where I taught radio. One of the projects I worked on at the WPA was with William Hastie(,) who was the head of the war department(,) and Noble Sissle. We put together one of the first coast to coast all black radio broadcasts, a play about the war sponsored by the War Department. Part of the dialogue called for the actors to speak in foreign languages. It was the first time that Blacks spoke in French, German, and Spanish over the airways.

"Being in the midst of so many talented artists, I managed to accumulate a valuable collection of art and folklore material from all over the world. Unfortunately, much of it was destroyed by fire or lost when Tony and I moved to California."

10

FRANCES IN CALIFORNIA

In 1941, Frances and Tony Hill left New York to vacation in Los Angeles. A few weeks earlier, Tony had written her a note that said, "I'm planning to go to the west coast for my vacation. If you want to come, you had better start saving your money." Ironically, at that time, she was the only one working while he had gone back to school for his master's degree. After quitting her several jobs, she hurriedly gathered together what she could, and they headed west.*

The train journeyed across the northern part of the country, near the Canadian border, past Lake Louise, and down the coast, winding inland. At each city in which the train stopped, they put in job applications. Just before reaching Sacramento, Tony got a telegram from Helena Coats, a friend they'd known in New York, telling them to get off the train. Knowing they were going to be passing through her hometown, Coats wired to have the train stopped in order to take Tony and Frances to the State Fair.

After spending two days at the Sacramento State Fair, they boarded another train for San Francisco where they planned to stay

*According to an article in Ebony Magazine "Ceramics by Tony Hill" (Vol. 2, Nov. 1946, pp31-35) in an interview with Hill, the U.S. Social Security Board did not appoint him field investigator because "they didn't think the country was ready for a Negro representative in a branch office." Frustrated, he quit his job. He goes on to say that Frances wanted to come to California to try the movies, so he came along.)

overnight before heading to Los Angeles. At the YMCA they tried to book rooms but were refused. Blacks were not allowed. With their usual flare, they chose the best hotel in the city, the St. Francis, in which to spend the night.

When they finally reached Los Angeles, Tony contacted his cousin who managed an apartment building on 43rd Street and Central Ave. where the couple stayed. After a few weeks, Tony decided to return to New York. Before leaving though, they agreed that Frances would stay in Los Angeles until he could wrap things up and join her there. He just knew she would be a big movie star and make lots of money.

With Tony heading back to N.Y., Frances searched for a place to live. When Leigh Whipper heard that Frances was looking for an apartment, he introduced her to the Stovalls. Whipper had relocated to Los Angeles and was living in Hollywood on Commonwealth.

Frances's eyes light up as she thinks of her friend from the Negro Actors' Guild in New York. She throws back her head and lets out a deep throaty laugh. She begins, "A very fine actor, Whipper appeared in many films including the original *Of Mice and Men*. He told me that when he first started acting on Broadway, he was given a little part with no speaking lines. For this he was paid three dollars a week which impressed him greatly.

"The next week the company did an All-American production with stars and stripes waving. The finale was so shockingly beautiful that everyone applauded enthusiastically. Leigh thought they were applauding him so he decided to ask for more money. He waited a while before approaching the producer. Just before he opened his mouth to ask a raise, the producer said, 'Listen, you damn fool! The next time people applaud the American flag, don't you take a bow.'

"The next time was at the opening of *Of Mice and Men* on Broadway. The set was just as beautiful. When the curtain opened and the audience applauded, Lee said under his breath, 'You're not going to get me this time.'"

Doctor Stovall, a well-known physician in Los Angeles, and

his wife had a home on Commonwealth, near Sunset and Vermont. Newly-built, their house was so modern that from time to time film companies used it for movie sets. The lot held two houses, the main house and a small guest house in the rear that had everything but a kitchen.

Because it was wartime, every evening at nine o'clock, the city imposed strict curfews and blackouts. "Because I'd never been in a situation like this before, the first thing I did was go out to see what was happening. The next day I got a special delivery letter from Tony that said, 'Darling, when the lights are out and they say it's a blackout, that's when you stay home!' I got so tickled that he knew me so well. He knew I would do just the opposite."

Meanwhile, Frances made contact with several of her friends from New York and Chicago, who were now in Los Angeles. One was Katherine Dunham whom she'd met through Tony. When Frances was doing *You Can't Take it With You,* in Chicago, Dunham came to see her many times. "She practically lived in my dressing room. I always say she went from my dressing room to the New York stage." Dunham had brought her troupe out from Chicago and was in rehearsal preparing to open at the Trocadero in Hollywood. Several wealthy nightclub owners were going to develop two night clubs in Hollywood - the big Trocadero or the Big Troc, for elaborate productions, and the little Trocadero or Little Troc for more intimate artists. Dunham was scheduled to open her production at the Big Troc but for financial reasons, the club never opened. The owners had planned to have her perform in the Little Troc instead, but her production was too big for the Little Troc. According to Frances, it was almost a fiasco.

"Katherine told them they needed a singer, not necessarily a great singer, but an attractive one. I suggested Lena Horne. Noble Sissle had introduced me to her when she was singing with his band in New York in 1940. Noble and I were engaged in conversation in Rockefeller Center when Lena walked up. I thought, 'What a beautiful person.' She was so radiant, her complexion gorgeous. I hadn't thought of her again until Katherine told me about the Trocadero dilemma. The Little Troc was exactly right for Lena. Her agent dressed the club with his stable of stars like Victor Mature, and Rita Haywood. Lena became the toast of the town."

After the Trocadero production fell through, Dunham decided to take her troupe on a road tour. An experienced organizer, Frances worked with Dunham getting the company together for the road tour, determining the kinds of boxes needed, organizing what went into them, deciding who was in charge of what, and how they could undo the setup quickly.

Not long after this, Ruthie Thompson, another New York friend, and Frances went down to see Ethel Waters who was rehearsing at the Biltmore theater. *Mamba's Daughter* was the play in which Ethel Waters made her dramatic acting debut. Waters played Hagar, Mamba's daughter. The role of Mamba was being played by Georgette Harvey.

The relationship between Frances and Ethel Waters had begun years earlier when Waters visited Karamu House. Frances admired Waters who was five years older than she. By 1939, Waters had achieved success as a singer and had appeared in musical theater on Broadway, in a concert recital at Carnegie Hall, and in nightclubs.

"Ethel said how glad she was to see me because she needed me especially at that time. She didn't tell me then what was wrong, though from time to time I'd stop by rehearsals and sense her dissatisfaction. There was a young woman who was in charge of stage managing *Mamba's Daughters*. I don't think it was as professionally done as it should have been.

"One day around five o'clock when I went by the theater to see Ethel, I found her in her dressingroom, quite upset. 'I don't have a costume. If I don't find one, I'll have to go out in my drawers,' she said. I located the wardrobe women who was also fit to be tied. They were using a new technique; one that I was familiar with from the summers in New York theater when I worked wardrobe. All the costumes were dyed several colors, one part green, another part brown, so that you had to know what went with what.

"This poor little blond couldn't figure anything out. I

managed to assemble enough for Ethel to wear. After that incident, Ethel wanted me around as much as possible. I was hired as her assistant, and I'm sure Ethel convinced the producers to offer me the part as Mamba's understudy."

"We started up the coast with the production. With the exception of the lights, everything ran smoothly. The light man was a very nice man except he was always getting drunk, so that whenever you wanted the spotlight in a certain place, he would be too drunk to get it right. Ethel would blow her top.

"She said to me one day, 'I know you have more than enough to do, but would you go see the light man and tell him for God's sake, give me my light where I should have it.' She asked me to stay with him for a while which I did. Tactfully, I told him that they couldn't get a production going if they didn't have the right lighting. 'I'll do the best I can,' he said. But I knew he wasn't listening to me. I went back and told Ethel, 'I think if you spoke to that man, he'll listen to you.'

"Ethel, probably one of the strongest women, not offensively strong, just the essence of strength, with great power with her God, went over to this electrician who was setting up lights for the evening performance. She looked at him and said, 'You know one thing? I'm going to talk to my Lord about you!' With his mouth hung open, this man, who was Catholic, turned orange, green, red, and blue and from that day on, he never missed another light beat. I'll never forget Ethel's power.

"Few people knew that practically singlehanded, Ethel, an ardent Catholic, financially supported a nunnery back East for years.

"She had a way of looking at you like some women I met later in Africa. For about two years, I felt Ethel's piercing eyes staring at me. Whenever I'd look up, she would be looking at me as if trying to put me on the spot. Evidently, I weathered it because we grew close, even going out to clubs and other places together dressed like 'successful madams,' as Ethel described us one time.

"So amazing was Ethel Water's personality that Vincent Price, when he wasn't on stage, stood in the wings watching her. During the production, Vincent and I had long conversations together. We found we had similar interest particularly in art. As a result of our friendship, when Tony and I brought Jacob Lawrence's exhibit to Los Angeles, Vincent who was a fervent patron of the arts offered the use of his gallery and became one of our major sponsors.

"When *Mamba's Daughters* completed its run in northern California, Ethel and I drove down the coast together. She sang all the songs of her childhood which her mother had taught her. Her favorite was 'His Eye is on the Sparrow.' We stopped off in Monterrey to spend two weeks at the home of actor Ramon Navarro."

Upon their return to Los Angeles, Waters bought a house on Sugar Hill as it was known then, an elevation between Western and Harvard north of Adams. Newly opened to blacks, the area had been under a "Restricted Covenant." Waters was one of the first to move in to the area. Shortly thereafter, three or four other blacks bought homes on the hill, including Juan Teasdale who played with Benny Goodman's band, and Ben Carter, the comedian.

Whenever black entertainers came to town, Waters would house them. Pearl Bailey stayed with her whenever she worked at a major nightclub in Los Angeles.

"Ethel offered me her third floor, a complete apartment. I knew she was strong, but I also knew I was strong, too, and that it would never work. We developed a good friendship so that when I did get my place, she gave me some nice furniture."

In 1951, while Frances was in Cincinnati for the National Negro Labor Council Convention, knowing that Water's birthday was approaching and that she was appearing on stage in *The Member of the Wedding*, in Chicago, Frances called up some friends they both knew in Columbus, Chicago, and Cleveland. She telephoned her old friend Garnet in New York. Garnet and Waters were close friends as well. She also called Butter Beans and Susie, and a range of people who had known Waters all her life.

"We all gathered in Chicago and my, was it cold! We bought tickets in the orchestra section, about three or four rows from the stage. It was a great experience. The emotion behind each line Ethel delivered, someone in the row knew from what experience she was drawing and would lean over and whisper 'that was from the time when Ethel....'

"Ethel was in Los Angeles when she first received the script from New York for Carson McCuller's play, *The Member of the Wedding*. She called me. 'Frank, you'd better read this script because I don't think I can do it. The young girl's crazy!' After reading the script, I told her that Frankie (the young protagonist played by Julie Harris) was innocent with all the problems of a young girl. 'You understand the script better than I do,' Ethel said. 'I'm going to write the author back and tell her to let you do it.' We could never work in a picture together because people thought we looked too much alike. "

11

PALM SPRINGS

Shortly after her return from her road trip, Frances left Los Angeles and went to live in Palm Springs, and for two years she worked in the hotels and health resorts there. It was a move that would have a lasting effect on her. Not only did she make contact with agents and producers vacationing there, but also, her community activism was reawakened.

"Uncle Buzz was my stepfather Ben's brother who had lived with us for a while. He never spoke above a low whisper, and when he did speak, his mouth didn't move. He was the darkest member of the Williams family and while the others were well educated, he was not. Uncle Buzz was one of the first iron pattern molders in the country. He had worked on Beach Bottom island where one of the country's first big iron mills was located. Uncle Buzz housed and fed all the iron workers. Every Saturday night, he set up a poker game. By the time the game was over, he'd won all the workers' money.

"One day as I was shopping in Central Avenue Market, I happened to glance across the room and not far from me stood Uncle Buzz, whom I hadn't seen since I was a young girl in Cleveland.

"Uncle Buzz owned a shoeshine stand in Central Avenue Market. Several years later, his business had expanded to where he owned several shoeshine stands. He needed to have an operation but he didn't want to leave his businesses because he didn't know of anyone he could trust to look after them. When I heard about this, I told him I'd manage them until he came out of the hospital. Dressed in brightly colored overalls, I shined shoes for months at his shoeshine

93

stand in Central Avenue Market until Uncle Buzz was able to resume his post. Tony's snooty friends, who already looked down on me because I was 'a show girl,' told him to speak to me.

"On this day, when I saw him I shouted, 'Uncle Buzz!' He turned and said, "My little Fanny, how are you, baby?' A large brown paper bag filled with half dollars, quarters, dimes, and nickels that he gripped in his hand suddenly burst and coins rolled everywhere.

"As I helped him pick up the coins, he told me that his daughter whose name, coincidentally, was Frances Williams, lived in Palm Springs and worked at the Murphy House, a health resort which specialized in warm, natural healing baths for 25 cents. Part Cherokee Indian, cousin Frances Williams built the first house on the Indian reservation where many of the black workers who worked in the resort city stayed. After talking with Uncle Buzz, I decided to move to Palm Springs and live with my cousin.

"For a while I worked with her at the health resort. Then I got a job at the largest hotel, the Lone Palm, where many wealthy patrons stayed. At night we would buy a case of beer and with the other workers, lay out under the dark sky, watching the shooting stars, and drinking beer. On my day off I would tag along with our next door neighbor who cleaned the pools at the homes of all the big producers, and swim while he worked.

"Whenever Tony came out to visit, he'd rent a bike, set me up on the handlebars and pedal all over Palm Springs. Occasionally, I would stand in line for a healing bath at the health resort with Paul Lucas, Adolph Menjou, and other Hollywood stars.

"At the hotel where I worked, I watched wealthy men sit around the pool all day playing gin rummy and exchanging thousands of dollars. On Saturday nights, their day off, the black workers would have their own poker game. Invariably, the police would raid the reservation, arrest the men and hold them over the weekend. When I learned of this I became so indignant I threatened to publicize the injustice of these raids. I made so much noise that the owners of the hotel offered me a raise to silence me. Eventually the raids stopped.

"One day, I received a call from a woman at the Desert Palms

Hotel asking me to come see her. The woman said she'd heard about the stand I had taken. She offered me a job as a waitress at her hotel. Not long after I began, I was put in charge of a hundred white waitresses.

"Working at the hotel, I got to meet many agents and producers. In particular, I became well acquainted with Bill Stein, founder of the William Morris Agency. Occasionally he would receive letters from France and because at the time I spoke French fairly well, he asked me to translate them for him.

"Meanwhile, Tony having wrapped up his affairs in New York, returned to Los Angeles. I joined him and we moved into a new housing project, Pueblo Del Rio Housing Project at 55th and Alameda."

12

_____

ACTORS' LAB

A lthough Frances had appeared in two of Oscar Micheaux's films in the 1930's, she saw herself as a stage actor and was reluctant to enter the world of Hollywood, particularly in the roles most black film actors were given at the time. Still she sought avenues in which to practice and perfect her craft. Actors' Lab was one. Even here, however, she encountered obstacles which frustrated and disappointed her.

The Actors' Lab was an excellent place for training, albeit its emphasis was on film rather than on stage training. Frances learned about Actors' Lab from Mary Tarsi who was in charge of the school. Among the actors attending at the time were Hume Cronin, Jessica Tandy, Bob Rosen, Kirk Douglas, Lloyd Bridges, Anthony Quinn, Shelley Winters, Howard Da Silva, and Nina Mae McKinney who rode with Frances to the lab every day. Many of the people at the lab had been members of the Group Theatre in New York.

The only black person on the staff, Frances took a full schedule of classes, and while most of the students had to pay for their training, she didn't because not only was she on the executive board, but also she worked lights, built sets, and handled wardrobe. Despite her involvement with the Lab, few acting roles came her way. With the roles she did get, more times than not, something would happen that would keep her from performing. Three incidents remain vivid in her memory.

Once she understudied Irene Tedrow who played a fortuneteller in a play called *The Wheel* with Keenan Wynn and Herd

97

Hatfield. Irene Tedrow was pregnant and when she went to the hospital, Frances, as her understudy, was supposed to take her place. Though she knew the part well, when the time came, they offered her a featured role in another play if she'd relinquish the fortuneteller one.

When the Lab did William Saroyan's *"The Son,"* she had a part but when she was called to New York, the director Diedrick replaced her with a white woman who went on to do it in the film version of the play. At another time, they decided to do a play called *The Birthday*. It was written by a woman, and since there were so few plays written by women, the Lab was anxious to do this one. Howard Duff was to play the lead. Jules Dassin, who later married Melina Mercouri, was the director. Frances had several good lines in the play.

She and Tony lived on Alameda and 55th Street in the new housing project. "To reach the Actors' Lab in Hollywood, I had to take three buses. If we worked late, I'd get home at 2 A.M. By the time I got home, after riding all the buses and waiting at the different bus stops, I'd be so tired and insecure." Despite the distance, for six months she braved the long bus trips back and forth to the Lab, making every rehearsal.

The script went through several rewrites. Gradually, she became aware that her lines were being cut, so that by the time of the performance, they had been reduced to "Good evening." Hurt and disgusted, she complained to the director.

"Don't worry, Frances," Dassin assured her. "I'll find a script for you to play lead." However, he never did.

With the exception of Karamu, Frances had had little opportunity to play lead roles; however, her skill on lights earned her recognition. In one production, unable to get a role, she was determined to do something. She worked the lights, probably the first time a black woman had ever done lights in Hollywood. It was challenging though not what she wanted to do. Nonetheless, she got more telegrams praising her light work than she ever got for acting.

Being on the executive board presented Frances with other frustrations. Her leadership ability and organization skills well-honed as a result of her work in Cleveland and New York, she had little tolerance for what she saw as mediocrity and hypocrisy. At a meeting of the board, there was a discussion about a play they wanted to do set in early New York City. The dilemma the board grappled with was how to raise money for the production. After sitting around for twenty minutes with no one saying anything, she grew impatient and suggested a simple fund-raising technique.

Someone said, "That's a brilliant idea. I think since this is your idea, you should chair the fundraiser?"

"I'm sure you do, but," she said, "how many Blacks are in the production?" As she suspected, there were none. Howard Da Silva glanced at her and smiled, "But Frances, the play is set in early New York."

"That was when my grandfather lived there," she responded emphatically. "For many years he had a shoe business in New York." She told them about Grandfather Nelson, her maternal grandfather. "There were lots of black people there, yet there are none in this play. I don't see why I should raise money for it unless you're going to change it."

She could feel the tension in the room as they shifted to another topic. Afterwards, a young woman came up to her and said, "I don't feel the way they do."

"Well, why don't you act like it?" she said. "I'm the one suffering. Don't ask me to be sympathetic with you when I don't know what your contribution is."

While she was stage manager, and on the executive board of Actors' Lab, an article came out in the *Los Angeles Evening Post* stating that the Actors' Lab wasn't as progressive as they thought they were because Negroes were noticeably absent from their productions. The board was so upset about the article, they called an emergency meeting. Hume Cronin, Howard DaSilva and other prominent actors were among those present. "We've got to answer this article," they said. "What are you going to say?" she said, as all heads turned towards her. "Everything they've written is absolutely true. Do you want me to tell you what has happened to me?"

For a long time after that, whenever she'd walk into the room, Howard DaSilva would say, "Here comes my conscience." Quite annoyed by that remark, she'd shoot back, "I'll be damned if I'm your conscience! Accept your own responsibility for your behavior and limited thinking."

She and DaSilva had known each other for a long time. An old friend, DaSilva began his career at the Cleveland Playhouse while she was at Karamu. When she lived with her brother, Bill over the marionette shop in an apartment with a rooftop garden, almost every weekend DaSilva would come and spend time with them.

On Monday mornings when she had to go downtown to a social workers' meeting, DaSilva would escort her to the yellow street cars, and say, "Have a good day, darling." He'd kiss her on the cheek. On the cars were black men and women going to work as maids, butlers, laundresses, and housekeepers who never knew what to make of this. To make matters worse, Frances wore jodhpurs, another strike against her because women didn't wear pants then.

When DaSilva first came out to California, he spent almost every weekend at her home bringing with him his girlfriend - later his wife-Jane.

More than once, she faced disappointment because there were just no parts for her at the Lab. To alleviate her frustration, she worked at everything else. Grateful for the solid foundation she got from Karamu and the Soviet Union, she worked on sets, lights, and costumes, whatever had to be done.

Despite the obstacles she encountered, Frances made endearing friendships at Actors' Lab. Jerry Fritz was a young man whose uncle was one of the best lighting technicians in the country. Though his uncle, who lived in New York, wanted him to take over the business, Fritz wanted to be an actor.

"Fritz and I worked together on the stage production of *Home of the Brave* starring Leo Penn. I was stage manager, Fritz did lights. I loved working with Fritz who always did an excellent job and never let me down. One day I asked him, 'Jerry, why don't you go into the technical end of the business.' 'I want to act.' He was adamant.

"The Lab planned to hold auditions for a new play which was a few weeks away. This would be Fritz's chance to find out whether he had any acting ability. To see what I could do to help him, I visited the classes one day and casually asked some of the instructors what they thought of Fritz who was attending their workshops. 'Jerry Fritz!' they all said. 'He hasn't got any balls.' Their attitude was so belittling. When I thought of Fritz's strong desire to become an actor and their sarcasm, I was disheartened. They destroyed him. I went back to the theater that night and asked him if he still wanted to act. 'Yes,' he said with determination.

'How much time do you have?'

'Mornings and a few evenings.'

'Can you spend the next few weeks at my house? Get some things together and come home with me tonight. I'll help get you ready for the audition.'

"Fritz had a clean but sloppy look. He wore moccasins that slipped as he walked, and he was just beginning to slouch. I analyzed him and found so much lacking, I thought, 'Good God.' There was so much to be done that it would be a challenge just to get him in the running.   "One of the first things I told him was to get new strong dress shoes and formal clothes. He slept in my livingroom and in the mornings we'd go for walks. As we walked, I watched him and suggested ways in which he could improve his posture. At the end of two weeks, you wouldn't think he was the same person.

"I knew he would be nervous as hell so I found a woman who would act as his partner for the audition. To get him secure and relaxed I told him, 'Jerry, this woman doesn't know much about theater and you know so much technically. Just before you start, when you go out, you'll have to make an adjustment to the lights in order to have the right kind of lights for your scene.'

"He followed my suggestions and won the audition. After that, he said, 'I don't know how to thank you, but I want to give you something I've made with my hands.' Early one morning he came over and built a bookcase for me which I still have.

"Later Jerry went to New York and fell in love with a wealthy

101

young woman who was an only child. He told her he wouldn't marry her until she came out to California to meet his mother. They came out to L.A. and stayed with me for almost a week. Upon their return to N.Y., they bought a beautiful three-story house in the Village and made over the top floor for me. When I was in *A Raisin in the Sun* on Broadway, I stayed there.

"In the 1960's Fritz became the treasurer of the director's union in television. By this time, I had moved to Mexico. Whenever he had questions concerning a union matter, he'd call me from New York to discuss it. Then one day I received the news that Fritz had died suddenly. It was a heavy blow."

Another person Frances met at Actors' Lab and admired greatly was actor/director Danny Mann. Because of his influence, she got to lecture twice at Lee Straussberg's School in New York. Mann had gone to war and when he came back, every line in his face said "war" to her. She was overwhelmed; it was the first time she felt she needed to apologize for not being there.

"That very night that I met him, he had to leave for New York where his parents lived. When he got there, he called me long distance. 'Frances, I cannot get you out of my mind. The way you looked at me, what did you see?' I was still so immersed in the profoundness of it all, I couldn't tell him. Never have I ever been so overcome with the meaning of war.

"A few years later, I had just come from a concert in Carnegie Hall in New York. It was two o'clock in the morning, and as I was walking to the subway, I noticed a man coming towards me. I was near the curb, he, near the building. Despite the hour, the streets were crowded. Just as we reached the same space, I recognized Danny, and he, me. Like two dancers with arms outstretched, we moved towards each other. It was so powerful. People milled around watching us probably wondering what was happening. He hugged me and told me he had recently gotten married and lived nearby.

"'You're coming with me. I don't care what other plans you've made. We're having breakfast together. I want you to meet my wife.' We stayed together until six that morning.

"The next time I saw Danny was in my home in Los Angeles when he came to my theatre to see a play with Paula Kelly and Roscoe Lee Brown. After the performance, we all gathered in my kitchen."

In addition to Actors' Lab, Frances worked with Charlie Chaplin at the Circle Theatre in the Round and at the Cosmos Theatre in Hollywood. The whole experience with Chaplin was very enlightening. She found that many of their views on the technical aspect of constructing plays contradicted others' on the board. When he decided to go to Switzerland, he invited her to go with him, but being a married woman, she declined. Turning down Charlie Chaplin was the one move in her life that she ever truly regretted. Much later she worked with Chaplin's son who was apprenticing at one of the acting studios.

Eventually, she began to get small parts in plays at the Lab to the extent that when she started doing film, Variety wrote, "Frances Williams is on her bicycle going from studio to studio to theater all in one day."

13

BLACKS AND HOLLYWOOD

" I've tried and I think many of us have tried to
make things a little better for the ones who
followed. It doesn't always work but you want
to make it a little better. You want to make them
realize that they must reckon with you
and that you are a human being."
Frances Williams

The script arrived special delivery. Her heart racing, her palms sweaty, Frances tore open the package. She was to play Amy, the maid in her Hollywood film debut, *Magnificent Doll*, a film about the life of Dolly Madison. It starred David Niven as Aaron Burr, Ginger Rogers as Dolly Madison, with Burgess Meredith, and Peggy Woods.

Eagerly she turned the pages scanning each part for her lines. It wasn't until she reached the last page that she realized she had hardly any lines. She thumbed through it again. By the time she got to the end, she felt her pressure rise. Damn mad! she slammed the script down on the table.

That night she could hardly sleep wondering what the next day would be like. She'd made two films with Oscar Micheaux but this would be different. This would be her first film for a major studio. Her friends at the Actors' Lab and Circle Theatre sent her all sorts of congratulations. Finally, she would be getting her feet wet. Now she would gain first-hand knowledge of what it was really like to be a black actor in Hollywood.

When she arrived in Los Angeles in 1941, it was not easy to cope with the situation she found there.   First of all, she didn't like what Hattie McDaniel and Louise Beavers were doing with those kerchiefs on their heads.   It was embarrassing. Secondly, she'd made up her mind years ago that she would not accept a part that called for her to speak in heavy dialect. She'd always refused before, and she wasn't about to start now; As a result, she turned down many parts and was in California almost five years before she worked in film.

Then one day, after much thought, she reached a decision. She had no right to criticize an industry of which she knew little, and with whom she was unwilling to become involved.   As long as she stayed on the outside, she was helpless to bring about a change.

In the spring of 1942, while she was living in Palm Springs, her old friend, Leigh Whipper, put her in touch with Walter Herzbrun who had a number of well-known actors as clients.   When Herzbrun called her in Palm Springs and said he was interested in representing her, one of the first things she told him was that she wouldn't do stereotyped roles.   Still, knowing it would limit her opportunities to work, he agreed to represent her.

Because Herzbrun's brother was artistic director at Universal Studio, he always got his scripts ahead of time. He knew what was coming out before everyone else did, and if he thought there was a part for her, he'd call. Meanwhile, she returned to Los Angeles and became active with Actors' Lab, Cosmos Theatre and the Circle Theatre until 1946 when she made her Hollywood debut in *Magnificent Doll* .

By morning her anger and disappointment had abated. She arrived on the set early, ready to do whatever she was called upon to do. The cast and crew greeted her warmly. Intrigued, she watched them work, blocking out scenes, rehearsing lines. Finally, Frank Borzage, the director, came over to her and told her to improvise her part.

In time, she learned that black actors were held in so little regard that frequently lines for them were not even included in the script. You were simply told to improvise, and that's what you did.

She followed Borzage's directions; whenever he wanted her in a scene, she improvised her lines which, because of her training, wasn't difficult. As the day progressed, she found herself much in demand. Each of the main actors wanted her in his or her scene to dress up their role.

Once she grew accustomed to improvising her lines, she began to look around for ways to fill out her character. They were shooting a scene about the evacuation of Richmond. The first time they did the scene, she simply ran as directed, carrying nothing. 'This is ridiculous,' she thought. 'The city is being evacuated and everybody is gathering up their belongings except me. I'm just supposed to run.'

She asked the prop man to bring her two blankets and some newspapers. Crumpling the newspapers up, she wrapped blankets around them so that it looked as if she were carrying all her belongings under her arm. As she made her way through the streets, bearing her bundle as if it weighed a ton, Niven, who was behind her, came up and whispered, "I can't let you carry such a heavy load. Give them to me," he said, taking the bundles. He was so surprised when he realized how light they were, he laughed.

Of all the members in the cast, she loved working with David Niven. Between shots he would hold the cast spellbound with his stories about the days when he was in the British army. Before he would begin a tale, he'd make sure she was included in the group. He'd call, "Bring a chair for Frances," and wait until she was seated.

Not all people were as gracious as Niven, though. Black actors had to face a lot of insensitivity and ignorance from some whites in the industry. For example, it was assumed that every black actor knew and could recommend a good cook, a reliable maid or chauffeur. Many times when Frances went on the set someone would invariably ask her, "Do you know where I can get a laundress." Or, "My cook just left. I wonder if you could help me find a replacement?" They never dreamed that she had studied in Europe, had appeared in many plays and had been the head of a theater movement in Cleveland. It was so insulting and difficult.

To react with hostility to these demeaning assumptions could cause more serious problems and jeopardize her entry into the film world. Frances was well aware of what had happened to her friend John Marriott, an actor who had been with her at Karamu House in Cleveland and who came out to Hollywood to do *Little Foxes* with Tallulah Bankhead in 1941. His part normally would have gone to Clarence Muse who it seemed got every other job available - boot black, porter, servant. Muse was well-liked. To succeed in his career, Frances felt, he used the technique of capitulation; in other words, he accepted the status quo.

In the *L.A. Sentinel*, Jan. 21, 1946, Muse defends the black actor who was under attack by the NAACP for the type of roles he/she accepted. He says "the technique of pressure must be well-planned in order not to put them out of business...[they] are not gangsters playing parts to destroy Negro dignity. They are earning bread like lawyers, doctors and workers."

The head of the NAACP, Walter White lashed out at Hollywood and the Negro actors and actresses who accept roles as "slavishly subservient menial or as a comic figure...What is more important - jobs for a few Negroes playing so-called Uncle Tom roles or the welfare of the Negro as a whole? If a choice has to be made, the NAACP will fight for the welfare of all Negroes instead of a few." (*L.A. Sentinel*, March 14, 1946)

In contrast to Muse, John Marriott, an extremely well-trained actor, had great dignity and may have been perceived by the crew as a potential rival to their old friend Clarence who never made waves. Whatever the reason, they purposely went out of the way to sabotage his career. According to Frances, the technicians adjusted the blinkers on the lights so that there wasn't one shot you could clearly recognize him. There is no doubt in her mind that it was because of this John never worked in Hollywood again.

Magnificent Doll taught her that there were different ways to fight for your dignity. When she came along, Louise Beavers,

Stepin Fetchit, and Hattie McDaniel were well-established in Hollywood.

Both Hattie McDaniel and Stepin Fetchit had their own way of fighting the racism they encountered. Hattie McDaniel, for one, made sure her family was employed in the industry. Despite the demeaning roles he played, Stepin Fetchit made a lot of money in film. He confided to Frances one day as they walked down Jefferson Boulevard, that few people knew that he had gone through three fortunes.

Because of her early social and political consciousness, Frances developed her own way of fighting. Some of the production people on the set of *Magnificent Doll* would tell vulgar stories. One of the grips, who it seemed, specialized in telling dirty stories, would tell them to her every time they'd meet, stories that embarrassed and nauseated her. Knowing what had happened to John Marriott on *Little Foxes*, she was reluctant to react without much thought.

For three or four weeks, every time he would tell a vulgar story, she'd counter with an honest personal story. Then finally, one day, with just a trace of sarcasm, she said, "You're such a wonderful raconteur. I'd love to hear you tell some personal stories about yourself." His mouth dropped open, his face turned red and as he slowly walked away, she thought to herself, 'Now I've done it. That's the end of my film career.' Finally when she had a break, he came over and said, "I want to apologize. I have never been so beautifully put in my place. May I buy you a cup of coffee?"

One thing that disturbed her during the filming was the complete absence of black extras. The Screen Extras Guild had black members who were almost never hired. In 1941, through her involvement with Actors' Equity, she had many meetings with those extras about this situation. The scarcity of jobs for them was so bad that Walter White, who was then head of the NAACP, came out to the West Coast in response to this.

It happened that Essie Robeson, Paul Robeson's wife, was out here, too. Robeson was doing *Sanders of the River* with Nina Mae McKinney, "a really terrible film that found my friend, the great

Paul Robeson, reduced to playing a stereotype as he did in almost every one of his films." Both she and Katherine Dunham were disgusted about it; but whenever they tried to reach Walter White, he had no time. Finally, hoping they'd get a chance to tell Essie Robeson and White what they thought of the film, Frances and Dunham invited both of them to dinner at Dunham's house knowing they wouldn't refuse.

Dunham and her artist husband, John Pratt, lived in a large house just off Sunset Boulevard. Frances cooked, and after dinner both she and Dunham let Essie Robeson have it with both barrels. They told her what they thought of Paul playing such a demeaning role. She responded, "You can say what you want, but Paul is getting an awful lot of money for it. If we have money, we have power." Frances wanted to strangle her then and there. Whether as a result of the dinner or not, Paul Robeson never did anything quite like *Sanders*... again.

White was just as bad. When Frances told him she would set up a meeting with the black extras so that they could discuss their concerns, he said, "I don't need to talk to those niggers." Without his help, black screen extras were finally able to work things out with the Screen Extras Guild, mostly through their organized protest.

One way they fought for inclusion was simply by making the industry aware of a film's historical inaccuracy. In her own way, Frances contributed to this effort. In one scene in *Magnificent Doll*, a plague was destroying the city. As the plague swept through Richmond, hundreds of people were carried out on stretchers. Watching all the white extras being carried out, Frances became increasingly annoyed. Knowing that Ginger Rogers had a lot of clout, she said casually to her, "Isn't it amazing that no blacks caught the plague? They must be a healthy lot."

"What did you say, Frances?" She repeated it. Ginger Rogers looked around in amazement. "You're right," she said finally.

After lunch, the director decided not to work on that scene until they had black extras. Not until the mid 1950's, though, were African Americans seen on a somewhat regular basis in contemporary crowd scenes.

Frances worked on *Magnificent Doll* thirteen weeks. At the end of filming, she made herself a smart-looking dark suede suit, and with musician Benny Carter as her escort, went to the wrap party. Usually at the wrap party, the leading actors would give presents to the technicians and crew members. Frances went over to the head technician and told him how much she appreciated everything he and his crew had done for her. She wanted to give them something for being so kind, but she didn't have much money. He shook her hand and smiled. "Miss Williams, you don't have to give us anything. It was a joy to work with you."

Whether or not Frances consciously set out to change the industry in her first film, subtle changes did occur. It was in her nature not to accept the roles in which she found herself placed, but to try to make things better as she did throughout her stage, film, and television career. Filling out a flat character, confronting ignorance, and pointing out historical inaccuracies, may seem insignificant, but it was a start.

14

―――

SECOND TAKE

L ater, that same year, she played Matillon in her second film role, *Her Sister's Secret*, directed by Edgar G. Ulmer and produced by Henry Brash. In 1949, she worked with James Mason and Joan Bennett in *The Reckless Moment*, produced by Walter Wanger and directed by Max Ophuls in his last American movie.

An intriguing storyline, the plot of *The Reckless Moment* evolved around a mother's attempt to save her daughter who has accidentally killed her lover. Frances played Sybil, the housekeeper. In a crucial scene, accompanied by Sybil, Lucia Harper (Joan Bennett) who is distraught by the whole affair, must follow Martin Donnelly (James Mason) to a spot where he can dispose of the body of a blackmailer. Rather than play her part the usual way, Frances wanted to do something different so she asked the director, "Why not let me drive the car instead of Joan?" It took three weeks for him to decide to let her do it. Once again Frances felt that by becoming more than a prop, she added something to the picture.

She had spent fourteen years at Karamu House appearing in eighty-five productions, studied theater in the Soviet Union for two years, played on Broadway and across the United States in *You Can't Take It With You*, yet in 1951, when she worked in *Showboat*, the first major problem she was confronted with was whether or not to wear a bandana. Two things she had already decided she would not do was to speak in heavy dialect or wear a bandana. She loathed bandanas.

While doing *Magnificent Doll* in 1946 part of her costume

113

called for her to wear a frilly French maid's hat. Having to improvise much of her part was bad enough, but to have to wear a frilly maid's hat was too much. When they got ready for her on the set, they couldn't find the head gear.

First, the wardrobe woman searched her dressing room for it unsuccessfully. Next a host of others came to search for the hat but to no avail. Lastly the director came up. He repeated their search. When he picked up her script and leafed through it, the hat fell out. He said, "You know, we sent all the way to France for that outfit." She glanced up at him sheepishly and shrugged, "I tried." After they all had left, placing the hat on her head, Elizabeth Searcy, her hairdresser, said, "Everything I put on you looks good." At least it isn't a bandana, she thought.

The first day on the set of *Showboat* the wardrobe woman presented her with a bandana and told her to put it on. She refused saying, "My character doesn't work in the field so there is no justification for me to wear a bandana." A few days later, the wardrobe woman approached her with another colorful bandana. "Don't you think this is pretty? Why don't you just try it on?" Again she refused.

At various times throughout the shoot, wardrobe would present her with yet another bandana, to her annoyance. All together, they presented her with seventeen kerchiefs. Each time, she declined their offer. Finally realizing she wouldn't change her mind, they stopped. In all the years since its Broadway debut and the hundreds of productions and two previous films, Frances probably was the first black woman to play the role without the traditional bandana.

Showboat starred Katherine Grayson, Howard Keel, Ava Gardner, Agnes Moorehead, William Warfield as Joe and Frances as "Queenie." William Warfield, who was once married to Leontyne Price, was well-educated and talented, with a great baritone voice. He had just completed a tour in Australia when he was brought to Hollywood for *Showboat* , his first film.

Frances, who was always aware of what went on around her, noticed that every time there was a break in the production, Warfield would sit down at the piano and clown. The white members of the cast were amused, but she found it really embarrassing that anybody had to work that hard to get attention. She didn't know how to tell Warfield he didn't have to clown for white people to find his place in the film industry.

Also, it seemed to her that Warfield acted very superior to all the other blacks on the set because he never associated with any of them. Frances prided herself on her relationships with everyone, particularly the workers. Whenever she was walking with the director or the producer, and she saw her fellow worker, she would say to the producer, "Pardon me, here's a friend of mine," and she'd go over to the worker and exchange greetings. "It's an investment because when you have the respect and a relationship with all the people, you always know what's going on."

Warfield's behavior disturbed her. Then one day, when she learned that Marian Anderson was coming to town, she saw an opportunity. Knowing how much Warfield admired Marian Anderson, Frances asked him to come with her to see Anderson perform. When the show was over, they went backstage. As soon as Anderson saw her, she said, "God, here she is again! Every time I look up there's Frances. I've seen her all over the world."

Frances had met Anderson in 1939 when she lived in New York and had since run into her in her travels. When Frances had lived in Finland, she and Anderson kept running into each other which resulted in their becoming very good friends. Whenever she would walk down the street in Finland, people would tell her that she reminded them of Marian Anderson. To Frances, not being compared to Hattie McDaniels but to Marian Anderson was a source of pride.

Still working on changing his attitude, Frances invited Warfield over to her house for dinner. Afterwards, she mentioned casually, "My hairdresser, told me to tell you not to wash your hair every day because it's bad for you." The hairdresser, Elizabeth Searcy, a black woman, had been with her on all her pictures. She was a smart woman; Frances admired her. Warfield was curious as to why Searcy didn't tell him directly. "Why don't you ask her?" Frances said.

On the set the next day, Warfield went over to Searcy and asked her about his hair. From time to time, Frances observed them talking. He still clowned around on the set a bit, but he seemed much more relaxed around others.

Frances felt that it was crucial that African Americans keep creating jobs; unfortunately, she also discovered there were times when they were responsible for eliminating some. When she came out to Hollywood, every black actress of importance always had her own hairdresser. Then it became fashionable for white hairdressers to do everybody's hair, though very few were equipped to do a good job on African American hair. The thing that hurt her, was that when very good actresses would come out from New York, Frances would try to tell them to "have your own hairdresser." Many ignored her. As a result, today, it isn't important to have a black hairdresser on the set even if there are a number of black actors in the film. "We lose jobs because we fail to help our own."

For the most part the cast of *Showboat,* like the cast of *Magnificent Doll* and the other films she had worked on, were a delight to work with. Every day, while on location, the cast and crew would gather in the commissary for lunch. Sitting at long tables they'd have lively discussions that ranged from politics to the economy. One day they were having a discussion and someone said something about the Nicholas Brothers. Frances said, "I think it's a damn shame that these fine black artists can't find work! They have to go to Europe. On top of that, even though they are working abroad, they still have to pay U.S. taxes. It's wrong!"

Joe E. Brown, who loved to tell jokes, was sitting nearby. In response to her remark, Brown, who Frances characterized as a right-wing reactionary, became almost apoplectic. She repeated it even louder and added, "Roland Hayes, Marian Anderson" - she listed all the other artists she knew who had to go to Europe to work - "And to have to be taxed because your country won't let you work, it's a damn shame!" He sputtered and threw daggers at her, but didn't say a word.

15

———

MANEUVERS

B y the late 1950's Frances had gained quite a reputation as a fighter. When *Porgy and Bess* was being made, the dancers, well-trained people, were being paid the same as extras rather than as professionals. According to Frances, instead of seeking help from Sidney Poitier or Dorothy Dandridge who were well-known actors with a certain amount of influence, the dancers came to her because they knew she would fight for them, even though she was not in the film. They were also able to enlist the aid of Sammy Davis, Jr., and together they fought to get paid a professional dancer's salary and won.

The problem of exploitation in Hollywood was not limited to African Americans. In the 1960's, when community theaters were springing up all over the country, Frances conducted a workshop with a group of 18 American Indians to help them get a core of people to organize their own theater. Among them was the youngest son of Jim Thorpe. Jack Thorpe told her stories about his father, one of which had to do with the time Thorpe was working on a picture in Hollywood. "All the Indians who were extras were being paid $3.00 a day, not even an extra's salary. Since at the time he had clout, Thorpe asked them if they wanted him to be their representative. "He went to the studio heads and told them that the Indians were not happy because they were receiving below the scale of extras. Wouldn't they consider raising their salaries? The studio heads said they wouldn't do that, but they had another idea. Instead of raising their salaries, they said they would give them guns to keep with all the blank

117

ammunition they needed. Thorpe responded, 'Give us real bullets and we won't ask you any more questions.'

This anecdote illustrates a strategy Frances used many times to gain attention within the industry. "You just have to find a way to get their attention, to shock them into being aware of your existence."

In 1951, the same year she worked in *Showboat,* Frances was sent out to Warners Brothers to audition for a part in *Three Secrets*. When she got there, the reception room was crowded. She took a seat and waited. On the table in front of her was a *Los Angeles Times* newspaper which she picked up and started glancing through.

"At that time, each issue had a rotogravure section, two pages of pictures of happenings around L.A. This particular issue featured the cotton industry in L.A. with a whole series of pictures on the industry. After examining all the pages very carefully, I noticed there wasn't a single black person anywhere. It was so brazen, I started to laugh. The more I thought about it, the funnier it got. Here was the cotton industry built on the backs of my people and there wasn't a picture of a black person in it, not pushing a cart, not loading a wagon, nothing. So I laughed and laughed. The people in the reception room looked at me as if I was crazy. I held up the paper and pointed. 'Look, look,' I said. Nobody else thought it was funny.

"But doors began to open, and other people came out to see what was going on. The producer and director came out very concerned. 'What's happening out here?' the producer said. I held up the paper, pointed and howled.

'It's about the cotton industry that was built on the backs of my people. Do you see any black faces on any of those pages?'

They shook their heads no doubt thinking that I was crazy. Then the director said, "Okay, come on into my office. You won that one.' When I was hired for the job, I suspect it was because of that incident since they didn't ask me anything about my acting background, and I didn't feel it was necessary to tell them. All they wanted was a black person to play the role of the housekeeper."

Having extensive training in the theatre and being an

118

observant person, sometimes Frances found herself torn between playing as ignorant as everyone thought she was, or revealing her knowledge. One day during production, as she watched them prepare to shoot a close-up, she noticed that they had taken down the wrong walls for the shot. Nobody else seemed to notice. At first, she thought, 'I'm not going to say anything. After all, I'm just a little black woman working here.' Finally, she couldn't stand it.

She went over to the director. "You've removed the wrong walls for the shot." "That's impossible," he said, brushing her off. He continued to set it up. Then, just before the cameras began to roll, he called for the crew to put back the walls and take down the right ones. Later, he came over to her and said, "You know how many thousands of dollars you saved us." He told her that she could see all the rushes on the picture any time she wished.

He didn't know her as an actress nor what kind of equipment she'd brought with her. These were the kinds of things she'd met with more than once. Rather than discouraging her, though, they made her stronger and helped her to develop a variety of techniques to survive in the industry.

Another time at MGM she had been announced by the secretary and sent in to see the director. "This man sat writing as if I wasn't there. He didn't say, 'Good morning,' or 'Kiss my foot.' He just went on writing with his head down not even acknowledging me or even asking me to have a seat. 'What do you do with foolish people like this?' I thought.

"Glancing around the room, I noticed on the wall behind him, a picture of a man with a halo that had dropped and had become a noose. 'When you moved into this office, was it already furnished or did you bring your own furniture?' I asked.

"Suddenly he stopped, and looked up at me. 'What?'

"'I said I was looking around the office and I wondered which of these things were your own or whether they were in the office when you came. For instance, that picture in back of you. I'm very impressed with it.' He said it was his. Then he apologized for keeping me waiting, asked me to sit down and we began to talk. I was hired on the spot."

16

—————

TONY

Tony loathed the idea of going to war. It made no sense to him. Regardless, when he received a letter from the draft board, he went down to the induction center with all the other guys. After a few hours, he came home and had me rolling on the floor with his descriptions.

"First, he said, the recruiter asked him all sorts of questions. Next, he was ordered to 'Take off all your clothes' and told to sit on an iron stool that Tony said was 'So cooooold.' The medical officer asked him, 'How's your bladder? Do you wet the bed?' 'Yes,' Tony said, 'every night.' He was miserable. Every question the man wanted him to say yes to, he said no and vice versa. Finally, they wrote him telling them they were sorry, but they couldn't use him." His contribution to the war effort was working in a plant making small parts for airplanes.

While he was working at an aircraft plant as a turret lathe operator, Tony and Frances lived in the Pueblo Del Rio Housing Project on 55th and Alameda where he met Glenn Lukens. A renowned ceramist, Lukens, head of the Fine Arts Department at the University of Southern California, was holding night classes, teaching housewives and war workers to make skillets, pots, and cups. Tony became interested and enrolled in Lukens's class.

Lukens lived on 5th Avenue near Adams in a beautiful house designed by the eminent architect Raphael Sorriano. Situated on a large piece of land, surrounded by a concrete wall, the house had high windows and an enormous fireplace. In his greenhouse, he grew

121

enormous melons and other plants that Frances said he fed soup.

A close friendship developed between Lukens and the Hills. They worked on various art projects, and whenever the Hills needed a place to hosts a large party, Lukens's house was always available. Upon the urging of Frances, Lukens, who was from Kentucky, went back there to purchase huge iron pots to put in his fireplace. Then she taught him how to cook there. Afterwards, he began serving meals from the hearth.

One time Lukens became seriously ill and had to get to the hospital. "He had this fabulous home with no one to care for it. 'Don't worry,' I assured him. 'I'll take care of your home and you.' I drove him to St. John's Hospital, and after registering him, the attendants prepared to take him upstairs to his room. Just as they began to wheel him into the elevator, the sister who was in charge approached. Seeing me, she said, 'Stop, Don't put that man on the elevator.' I turned to her and said, 'He is not a black man. He is white so you can let him go ahead.'"

Being the head of the Fine Arts Department at the USC, there were times when Lukens entertained important people such as the mayor and the governor. Often because his house was so modern and had such a large yard, Frances and Tony gave parties there.

In 1946, they hosted a farewell party for Countee Cullen at Lukens's house. Cullen had been in Hollywood and was on his way home. Right in the middle of the party, he received a call that his father was very ill, so he left early and flew to New York. Ironically, instead of his father dying, Countee Cullen died shortly after.

Tired of living in the projects, Tony began looking for a house to purchase. He found one on 37th Place between Western and St. Andrews for $2600. It stood on a huge lot on which grew four apricot trees. Not only was the house too small, but also, it was poorly constructed. It had a kitchen with a small place for eating and another room which they used as a combination diningroom and livingroom. They bought some coffee tables on which Tony placed pieces of marble, he said, "to keep the wind from blowing the house away."

A short time later, Tony found another house at the end of 5th Ave, near Exposition, which at that time was a dead-end street. The house sat at the back of a large lot. Just beyond was a beautiful little park. Frances didn't think they could scrape up enough money to buy it, but after Tony threw a temper tantrum, she gave in. They paid $4600 for the house. The walls were covered in a wallpaper pattern of blue ribbons and roses; it was unbelievable! A young black couple had recently bought it. Soon after, they separated and decided to sell the property and divide the proceeds.

Frances and Tony did the entire house over. First they stripped off the wallpaper. Next Tony went downtown and brought bolts of material from which she made drapes. From someone in his ceramic class, Tony got some custom-built furniture. Finally, he made lamps and ashtrays.

No sooner had they finished redecorating, when Tony decided that they should have a party. Frances invited her friends, and he invited his. She baked a ham, cooked a large pot of spaghetti, made a salad and served it with French bread and wine. About five hundred people came, filling the house to capacity.

When it was over, having made all the drapes the day before, and having done all the cooking, she was left to clean up. At that time in Los Angeles, the fog would become so thick and heavy, you couldn't go out after midnight. Because of this, many stayed over, even though they had very little furniture on which to rest comfortably. Tony, however, was gone.

Among their guests at the party was a journalist. William Cummings, a tall, blond, bespectacled, English man with a quiet demeanor. He was the publisher of NOW, one of the first weekly interracial magazines. When Frances awoke the next morning after the party, Cummings, who had gone home before the thick fog set in, was in the kitchen washing the dishes. No one ever locked doors in those days. "I knew you'd have to do this, so I took the day off to help." He washed every dish while she made breakfast.

All of their parties were like that first one. Their guest list included Louise Beavers, Hattie McDaniel and her brother, Lena

123

Horne, Anthony Quinn, and Lloyd Bridges. Everyone who was anyone came to their parties. The saying around town was that "If you haven't been greeted by Tony and Frances, you haven't been greeted." They gave parties just because both loved to entertain.

When the *Anna Lucasta* cast came to Los Angeles, Frances threw a party for them, and for the Delta Rhythm Boys, "very handsome young men, all college graduates. People came and came. I didn't know what to do. That evening, the house was so crowded the walls were throbbing. I asked Lena Horne to step out onto the patio with me. I knew she was the only one who could draw the people outside.

"At that time, Lena, who had recently married Lenny Hayton, told me, 'That man knows more about my people than I do. He's taught me so much.' Lenny was a very good Scrabble player. Many times he and I would play Scrabble until 5 A.M. at my house."

Frances gave book parties to introduce the publications of black artists to the black community. One featured Shirley Graham, W. E. B. DuBois's wife. She organized one at her house for Langston Hughes when one of his books was published. It was the only time she and Hughes had an argument. He expected it to be at the Hugh Gordon Book Shop, one of the most outstanding book stores this side of New York. It was run by Adele Young, Carmen DeLavalade's aunt.

Instead of having it there, Frances decided to have the book party at her house. Hughes told her it was one of the best book parties he had ever had. Everyone, including Hughes, took turns reading from his latest publication, and over 500 books were sold. Along with the readings, Frances served some good food, as had come to be expected.

Later, she had parties, fundraisers, some type of event in her yard almost weekly, including one of the last big parties for the Black Panthers.

* * * * * * * * * * *

In the mid-forties, Frances, along with a woman named Nash

- who was a very fine organist, singer and voice coach - decided to rent a studio where they could work almost full time with groups in acting and singing. The studio was owned by the Spikes Brothers, a group of brothers who many years earlier had a music store on Central and Twelfth street before they bought this studio at Jefferson near Normandie.

Frances and Nash brought in dancers, musicians and other artists to the studio. One in particular, Thelma Street, who was a versatile artist, danced there. "Originally from San Francisco, Thelma was one of those rare talents. She had big ugly feet and though a great deal of the time, she was ill, she could dance, compose music, paint - she did primitives mostly, that were so good, when she hung her paintings every child who came to the studio would try to imitate the dancers in the paintings. Thelma composed symphonies that were so good, the San Francisco orchestra played them."

During this time, there were few places in Hollywood where black and white musicians could play together. Frances discussed the situation with Norman Granz, who edited film at Warner Bros., and told him about her studio. One day, after talking about it for some time, he visited the studio and together they decided to host Sunday jam sessions there. Some of the musicians who played at the studio were Barney Cassel, Red Calandar, and Nat Cole. "The place became so popular that art students from nearby USC came to sketch the interracial crowd."

Later the jam sessions were moved to downtown Los Angeles to the Philharmonic on 5th Avenue across from the Biltmore Hotel. In 1947, Norman Granz Jazz at the Philharmonic featured jazz greats like Coleman Hawkins and Bill Harris. Then, Granz took the musicians on the road, to Europe and other places. However, once again, Frances chose to stay home with her husband. If she had gone, she speculated, she would have made millions managing the production. Among the items she acquired from her collaboration with Granz was her first mink coat. Granz went on to start an agency and became Ella Fitzgerald's manager.

When they did cultural things together, Tony and Frances

125

were a good team. They used the studio to exhibit the art of Jacob Lawrence, the first formal art exhibition of its kind in Los Angeles. With the help of Glenn Lukens, who did a Herculean job, they set up the exhibit and developed a list of sponsors which read like a who's who in modern art. Among the sponsors were Vincent Price, Ernest Biberman, Lipshitz, and some of the greatest artists from New York to California. The exhibit was so well attended, they kept it up for six weeks.

When Charles White came to Los Angeles, though Frances had never met him in New York, she knew of him. Someone asked her if she would set up an art exhibit for his introduction to the west coast. She talked to Lukens about it and he made available to her the art department at USC for White's first exhibition. On opening day, they had over 500 visitors, something unheard of at that time.

The last major art exhibit she and Tony brought out to California featured black artists from Washington, D.C., Boston, and the Metropolitan Museum in New York. That too, was successful. Though it was a great experience, it took so much work, they decided to turn the entire project over to a group of teachers who were interested in putting together not only art, but also poetry and other things. It became an annual event.

* * * * * * * * * * *

RUTHIE THOMPSON

Tall, with beautiful brown skin and long hair, Ruthie Thompson was a tremendously impressive woman and much in demand all over the country for her clairvoyance. Frances met her when she and Tony lived in New York. Ruthie was a close friend of Garnet's and Tony's. Also she was Ethel Waters's personal psychic and friend. When Ruthie moved to Los Angeles, many actors and directors in Hollywood became her clients.

Ruthie couldn't work with Frances, but she could with Tony whom she was very fond of; he loved her, too. They were in sync.

For example, Tony had friends in the army in the Pacific theater. When he and Frances would stop by Ruthie's house, she'd say, "Tony, have you been home? You have a letter in your mailbox from so and so." Then she would recite what was in the letter and sure enough when they got home, the letter would be exactly as she said.

Another time when they visited Ruthie, she said suddenly, "Tony, what's that all around you?" "Ceramics," he answered. "That's what you're going to be," she predicted. Tony became a renowned ceramist earning a great deal of money from his creations.

After studying with Lukens, Tony, who mastered everything he tackled, became quite proficient. Tony and Frances started a business creating functional ceramics. He made lamps for modern offices that could be set on coffee tables. Frances did all the wiring. To match the lamps, he made huge ashtrays. Then he hired a Japanese woman who was very good at making lampshades. Eventually, he took on a partner, Wilmer James.

When they wanted new shapes, Tony would get into his little Ford Roadster, and drive down alleys before the garbage was picked up and rummage through the bins to find all sorts of mad shapes. Frances would follow the trash trucks to where buildings were being torn down and pick up many odd things.

With the business growing like a house afire, they moved his studio from Long Beach to a building on Jefferson and Twelfth Ave and bought several kilns. Because of the restrictive covenant, they had to have a white friend rent it in her name.

It wasn't long before Tony gained the reputation of being one of five best ceramists on the west coast. His work was featured in the MGM movie *Holiday in Mexico*. Pieces sold in Argentina, Sweden, Canada, Hawaii, Panama, Mexico and almost every large city in the U.S. (*Ebony Magazine*. "Ceramics by Tony Hill" Vol. 2, Nov. 1946 pp. 31-35)

When he messed up a piece he was working with, if it didn't come out like the others, instead of charging less for it, he increased the price because, he said, there would never be another like it.

Then, at the height of his success, Tony and Frances

separated. Among other things, two incidents precipitated their breakup. One of the first big parties he gave was for the opening of his studio on 12th and Jefferson. Frances learned of the party from Essie Robeson. She went over to the studio and blocking her entrance was her old friend and roommate from Chicago, Lillian Sommers. Deeply hurt, she turned away. Riding home on the streetcar, she suddenly became aware of clenching the strapped so hard, she thought it would break. She had imagined her hands were around Tony's neck.

Shortly after that incident, she discovered he had saved a large amount of money with which he planned to take a trip to Mexico without her. She found his clothes and other items hidden beneath sheets, behind the piano, everywhere, and when she confronted him, he couldn't lie. He had never been able to lie to her.

Just when she was ready to tell him that they just couldn't make it, he was diagnosed with stomach ulcers. She thought, "I just can't put a man out who is sick." She lived several blocks from the grocery store and because the car wasn't running, she would walk the long blocks carrying all the things he needed, like milk and cereal. It took six pots to cook his meals, but she wouldn't let him leave until his stomach healed.

The Halpin family, who owned furniture shops all over town, had given Tony a lucrative contract; he could depend on a monthly income of $1,500 to $3,000. He supplied lamps for all their furniture displays. Frances learned later that they had given the contract to Tony because of her. When the Halpins learned that Tony and Frances had divorced, they cancelled the contract.

After Tony left, Frances became quite ill and had to take to her bed. Despite her ill health, she trudged to the store and one day, on her way back, her neighbor, Mrytle Pitts, took her packages from her, accompanied her home and cared for her until she was on her feet. It was the beginning of a long and close friendship.

* * * * * * * * * * *

PERCY LLOYD or P.L.

Shortly after she and Tony separated, Frances received word that her oldest brother P.L. had been killed in an automobile accident. P.L. had become pretty well off and had purchased a four-story mansion in Cincinnati, once the family home of William Howard Taft located on William Howard Taft Hill. The three top stories had fireplaces, and plumbing for kitchens and baths. Her youngest brother, Bill, lived on the top floor.

On weekends, the house was filled with guests including P.L.'s close friend, heavyweight champion Joe Lewis, with whom he often played golf. They would go hunting and bring in game which Cora, P.L.'s wife, would have the butcher cut up and she would prepare elaborate meals consisting of several courses served with the proper wine. Added to the decor was vases of fresh flowers.

The house was filled with antiques of which Cora was quite knowledgeable. Frances was fascinated with a mangle - a special kind of ironing board that pressed sheets, tablecloths, and linen - and the dryers that looked like big metal boxes with drawers inside which held rods on which you could hang clothes.

Brother Bill lived on the third floor where P.L. and Cora kept their winter clothing, furs and other storage items. One weekend during a visit, Frances remembered Bill had a birthday coming up. She decided to turn a section of the third floor into an apartment for him. She ordered everything he needed to make up an apartment. Actually they had so much furniture there already- bamboo tables and chairs, breakfast sets, everything except stove, refrigerator, and draperies.

Frances brought some yellow percale sheets and made curtains. She turned one of the rooms into a bedroom. It already had a fireplace and bathroom. She created a kitchen area and put in a refrigerator and stove. At two a.m., when Brother Bill opened the door and saw the entire apartment lit with candles, the table laden with food, and all his friends, he was so surprised, he turned around and went back out.

MEET IT, GREET IT, AND DEFEAT IT

P.L. and Cora threw a big party for Frances when she came back from Europe. All his accountants and other people were there. As she danced with one man, he would tell her things she'd done in Europe. Then she would dance with another man, and he would tell her things about her European adventure, she had almost forgotten. This went on and on until she discovered that P.L. had passed her letters around to his friends to read so that everyone knew more about her than she could remember herself.

"JOHN"

"When P.L. died he had forty honorary pall bearers who belonged to a country club in Kentucky. Each pall bearer told a story about him or one of the last stories they all had shared together.

"One story told was about a black man who worked like a slave on a plantation in the South. Though he wasn't paid very much, because of his labor, the place became very profitable. Having every thing they wanted, the owner and his family took a trip to Europe. Shortly after their return, the owner asked John, 'Don't you want to go on vacation? We've had such a good time and you've done all the work. We think it would be good for you.'

"John said he didn't know where to go. They said, 'Why don't you go to some place like Chicago? It's a big city and you'll find some people there you'll enjoy.'

"They eventually talked him into it. They decided on the hotel where he would stay and promised to send him a certain amount of money each week. John never learned to read or write, but he could recognize letters. They devised a message system so that they could reach him when they needed to.

"Finally, John went off to Chicago. He'd never seen any place like this. It was so fast, he was amazed by all the people and the traffic. He got to the hotel and was almost afraid to go out. Then he met a woman there, and this chick decided, 'Well, here's a real free bee.' She stayed with him and used his money buying clothes and living it up. This went on for four or five weeks until one day she came back from a shopping spree. He said, 'I gotta go home now.' She said, 'How do you know?' 'I got this telegram today,' he said and handed it to her. It said, 'MMMMMF.' 'What does this mean?' she asked. 'Don't you know?' he said. 'No,' she said. 'It says, 'Meet mule Monday morning, Mother Fucker.' I have to catch the train and get back.'"

In 1965, P.L. and Cora's daughter came out to Los Angeles to live with Frances. Lonnie hadn't been there long when Watts exploded. Frances's only niece was one of the first people killed in the uprising.

17

___

POLITICS AND THE COMMUNITY

As a teenager, Frances had worked with the Democratic Party and the Future Outlook League in Cleveland. When she went to the Soviet Union in 1934, she wasn't very politically aware to the degree that she felt she should have been, and while she learned a lot of things there, she was not immersed in politics. Though she'd done a lot of civic things in her youth, and had worked with Actors' Equity in New York, her political awareness broadened considerably shortly after she came out to California in 1941.

One incident that pricked her consciousness was when she met a group of black school teachers who had just come back from Japan. They brought back huge menus they'd gotten from the ship and reported that they didn't understand why at a certain time in the evening, the ship would turn off all the lights.

"I doubled up with laughter that these foolish women didn't realize that there was a war going on and the blackouts were for safety. They were all so pretty in their fine hats that it was shattering that these women who were supposed to be the heads of society could be so stupid. Their behavior made me want to be political. It was a matter of being fully alive."

However, it wasn't until the late 1940's that she became actively involved with progressive people. Being a member of Actors' Equity, she got on committees and worked with a lot of progressives doing whatever was needed, including preparing food. She worked with Indians from India, and Asians. An East Indian group and their mentors met at intervals at her house. She became treasurer of the organization.

When Harry Bridges came out to Los Angeles to raise money for the longshoremen's union of which he was the head, a group of actors from the union decided to have a fundraiser for him at the home of Bob and Sue Rosen. "I don't know how I became involved; however, I admired him for the work he had done with the union, getting them fringe benefits and other things."

Plans for the fundraiser were almost complete with one exception. They needed a featured performer. At one meeting Frances attended, she suggested they ask her old friend Katherine Dunham to be the featured guest. Everyone agreed. She contacted Dunham who consented to perform. The evening was a success. For other fundraisers, though she never had enough money to contribute, she worked hard and "cooked like a fool."

The Actors' Lab had a lot to do with raising her consciousness, as well. There, she was exposed to some of the finest political people in the arts. Unfortunately, she found them limited. Their limitations frustrated her. "We all live in our own space, however, I've been able to include a broad spectrum of people in my life.

"One day I was working in the kitchen and a voice said, repeatedly, 'It's your people that need you...These people will find their way. It's your people that need you. ' It finally hit me that I was helping these bunch of white people when it was my people that needed my expertise and guidance."

She did not have far to look. The local Black newspaper, the *L.A. Sentinel*, carried articles about the problems facing the Negro in the city. Housing shortages, job discrimination, inadequate police protection, police brutality. Within her own community, which was then under a restrictive covenant as were other cities across the nation, Frances found much to be done.

Most black Angelenos were crowded into housing on the east side of the city, around Central Avenue, in Watts, and in the Willowbrook area. One article quoted statistics that said that "Negroes [are] barred from 96% of the privately built war housing." (*L.A. Sentinel,* Jan. 1946)

It was difficult, if not almost impossible, for minorities to rent apartments or buy houses in certain areas like Crenshaw or Leimert Park. Though world famous, Nat "King" Cole faced the restrictive covenant when he and his new bride Marie Ellington purchased a home in the Hancock Park area of Los Angeles.

White residents signed petitions upholding exclusion of other races from their neighborhoods. If you wanted to buy a house in those areas, even if you were allowed to, you were charged exorbitant prices. And because the Ku Klux Klan was strong and active, minority residents were regularly harassed.

In Leimert Park, for example, a few miles south of where Frances lived, live rats were thrown into the homes of new black homeowners, and whenever they were away, their homes were flooded. Fire bombings, cross burnings were regularly reported, not just in Los Angeles, but also in Palm Springs, Big Bear, and Fontana where in Dec. 1945 the home of Mr. and Mrs. O. Short was burned and four members of the Short family died." (L.A. *Sentinel* , Jan. 1946)

Though the NAACP was active in other parts of the city, they were seen by some as ineffective. In response to the problems faced by the city's black citizens, many urged the organization to take action. An editorial in the *L.A. Sentinel* (March 1946) urged the NAACP to call "a two day conference for consideration of these conditions which threaten our community, our homes, and our lives." A $1,000 reward was offered "for the perpetrators of the bombings and attacks on the city's Negro citizens."

There were a few blacks living in the West Adams community, which included an area known as Sugar Hill when Frances and Tony moved there in 1943 - black professionals in the entertainment industry and in business, like the Nicholas Brothers, and Eddie "Rochester" Anderson, Ethel Waters, Ben Carter, Hattie McDaniel, Louise Beavers, Mitchell Myers, Noble Sissle, Andy Rosseau, and Ivan Houston who was president of Golden State Insurance Company.

Sugar Hill, according to an article in the *L.A. Sentinel*, was "stamped as a movie community because celebrities such as

135

MEET IT, GREET IT, AND DEFEAT IT

Ben Carter, Hattie McDaniel, and Ethel Waters were the first to make themselves veritable 'guinea pigs' in an attempt to live according to the theory of Americanism, where one chooses in the search for comfort." (Jan 10, 1946)

A group of concerned neighbors gathered at Frances's home one weekend to discuss their dissatisfaction with the situation in the community. Among the things they discussed was the restrictive covenant and other community problems such as the high prices being charged to new home buyers. One of the results of the meeting was that they decided they needed to set up workshops to educate prospective buyers.

They rented a hall, and invited five of the city's major black lawyers, including Hugh McBeth. Previously, new home buyers would file suits individually against the sellers who charged exorbitant prices. Because most lawyers charged heavy fees to try cases individually, it almost broke those who sort redress. The lawyers were asked if they would take on the cases collectively, pool their resources and charge one fee, but, according to Frances, they refused.

Not until 1953 was the restrictive covenant ended. In a decision by the Supreme Court on June 15, 1953, "a racial restrictive covenant could not be enforced at law by a suit for damages," a method used by organized white property owners against anyone who sold his/her property to a minority. (*Caucasians Only* by Clement E. Vose. Berkeley: University of Calif. Press, 1959. pg. 233.) No longer under threat of being sued for violating the covenant, Whites who wanted to sell their property were now free to sell to whomever they chose.

In order to protect the property of the black homeowners in Leimert Park, the Homeowners Protective Association organized by Charlotta Bass, conducted twenty-four hour patrols. In addition, the H.P.A. did a lot of work to keep Charlotta Bass's newspaper, *The California Eagle*, solvent, hosting benefits to raise money. Along with the *L.A. Sentinel*, *The California Eagle* was a major newspaper in the community.

In addition to problems with housing, minorities were not

welcomed in some of the neighborhood stores like Ralphs', Van de Kamp, Thriftys', nor the banks. To counteract this, they set up picket lines around these stores and banks. It wasn't until several years later when Boys Market came into the community and made gestures of friendship such as putting up huge signs in different languages that the people of the community felt welcomed in the store.

The next fight confronting the community activists was to break down the hiring practices of the places where Blacks could spend their money, but could not work. These same neighborhood stores would not hire Blacks or any other minority. To confront this problem, again the activists set up picket lines around the stores until they agreed to change their hiring policies.

Eddie "Rochester" Anderson, the actor who played Jack Benny's butler, lived not too far from where Frances lived. On the corner of Arlington and Jefferson stood a neighborhood market owned by Sam Newman. Though the population of African Americans was on the rise, no blacks worked there. The group of community activists decided to set up a picket line to urge Sam Newman to hire black workers.

While they picketed and held meetings on getting the store personnel integrated, according to Frances, Anderson supported Sam Newman. "After the fight which we won, whenever I'd drive into the parking lot, Sam Newman would come out, open my car door and give me a big greeting. Unfortunately, he didn't show that kind of respect for Rochester."

According to Geri Branton, the only group that joined the protest and underwrote their cause was the Communist Party. However, because of the support of the Communist Party, many people were afraid to become involved. They did not want to be connected with the Party. Branton, once married to Fayard Nicholas of the famous Nicholas brothers dance team, and long-time friend said, "Frances was not afraid. She was a great motivator. She brought people together."

Prior to their breakup, with so much happening around them,

137

Tony and Frances had a long discussion that lasted several days about which one of them should get actively involved. She had been grooming him to run for public office, but he wasn't interested. Finally, they decided that since Frances was an actress, she had less to lose than he. Besides, she had good organizing skills and a lot of political savvy.

In 1948, when her friend Myrtle Pitts asked her to run on the Progressive Party ticket for the California State Assembly for the 63rd district, in Los Angeles, Frances readily accepted. Her friend, Paul Robeson, was the co-chair of the "National Wallace for President Committee." Fay Blakensburg was the campaign manager, and Elinor Kahn, the state director. (*L.A. Sentinel* Aug. 12, 1948) Mr. Roberts was the Democratic incumbent, Gus Hawkins had just begun to run on the Communist ticket.

When Tony first learned his ex-wife was running for office, he told her campaign organizers, "She's too moral to be involved with politics." Though they were divorced, that he supported her campaign meant a lot to her.

Frances had never been one to back down from a challenge. From community work to the political arena wasn't such a great leap. Dorothy and Henry Krause agreed to help run her campaign. Both had worked in the early days to develop the Congress of Industrial Organization (CIO). Their friendship went back to the days when Frances was at Karamu House in Cleveland. Frances's platform included

-reestablish price controls and roll back prices to 1945 levels.

-pass a State rent control bill.

-support State housing initiative for 1,000,000 low-cost homes for veterans and non veterans.

-resume a slum clearance program.

In the area of civil rights, her platform called for

- guaranteed fair employment

- an end to discrimination and segregation in public places.

- an end to witch hunts.

138

"Stop Tenney witch hunts, loyalty checks, etc., which are spreading terror among the people."

- end police brutality.

-end the sales tax and eliminate tax on incomes below $5,000.

-establish permanent State-supported nurseries with means test as condition of entrance.

For labor, her platform urged:

- defeat anti-labor bills of Taft-Hartley type that were pending.

-guarantee minimum wage of $1.00 per hour.

-reaffirm Constitutional right to strike and picket without limitation.

She supported the program offered by Henry A. Wallace that demanded "a return to sanity and peaceful relations among nations."

Dorothy Krause, who headed Frances's campaign, got together a group of dedicated workers including pianist Bobby Short, and they went to work gathering support. They set up public meetings whereby Frances could make her position known. To dress up some of the affairs and increase the crowds, some of the Hollywood writers who were later blacklisted were invited to speak about their experiences.

Frances's biggest challenge, however, came when she had to make a speech. She asked Henry Krause, who was a writer, if he'd write her speeches. He said, "Of course, I'll help you. You write it out and I'll edit it for you." "Hell, I can do that, " she thought. Then she asked another important writer, and he said the same thing. This went on and on until finally she decided she would have to write her own speeches.

The first one she wrote made her ill. "I had to crawl all over my house on my hands and knees and pull myself up. I was a nervous wreck, I could not stand straight." Reflecting on her efforts, fifty years later, she said, "My advice to all is "don't give up hope if you're afraid of speaking. You can write your own speeches. If I can do it, anyone can."

Once she was asked to speak for ten minutes at the "Women for Wallace" luncheon. 'Only ten minutes. That will be easy,' she thought. The room was filled with well-dressed women in colorful hats and matching gloves. As she passed the president of the organization, on her way to the podium, the woman stopped her and whispered, "You can speak for an hour because we have enough time." She took a deep breath, a sip of water, and began. The hour passed so quickly, she felt she could have gone on for twice as long.

The California Eagle, May 20, 1948, reported on a three-way debate sponsored by the Bill Bernstain and Leimert Park chapters of the American Jewish Congress. G. Delbert Morris, the Republican candidate for the 63rd Assembly district, didn't show up. The Democratic candidate Sam Whitworth was outclassed by Frances. Her speech, "We want an America where no child can go hungry in the midst of plenty...where friends and neighbors can live in peace and security regardless of race, creed, nationality or color...freedom of speech, thought, press and religion...an America not for a few but for all of us..." was received with prolonged applause and characterized as a "one-way landslide." Frances went on to denounce the Mundt-Nixon Bill.

In August the Progressive Party led a boycott against high meat prices. Frances, along with Maynard J. Omerberg, candidate for Congress for the 15th District, led the boycott directed not at the neighborhood storekeepers, but against rising meat prices.

The *L.A. Sentinel*, one of the leading newspapers in the black community, came out in support of the Republican candidate for president, Governor Thomas Dewey. They predicted defeat for Henry Wallace saying that while "his platform was admirable, in many respects, [it] is only a smoke screen for behind-the-scenes promotion of a foreign policy that reflects the needs and desires of the Russian foreign office rather than the welfare of the American people." (*L.A. Sentinel*, Oct. 28, 1948) On the other hand, *The California Eagle* supported the Wallace campaign.

Democratic candidate President Harry Truman won the election receiving overwhelming support from the Negro community who voted a straight Democratic ticket. On the local level, though she didn't win the elections, Frances made a strong showing. On the night following the campaign, the organizers threw a big party at her house. The next day she headed to Mexico with Bobby Short.

* * * * * * * * * * *

BOBBY SHORT

After the election campaign, Frances was so tired and exhausted she told Bobby Short that she needed to get away.

The only place she could think of was Mexico. Short had recently been given a new Imperial automobile and he suggested they drive down together. The very next morning after the party, they started out.

"When we got near the border, I said, 'Bobby, I want to explain something to you. I know you're a child protege which makes you a star and you're a great artist. Don't pull any temperament on me because I am an actress and there isn't anyone who can display more temperament than me if necessary. So understand, we aren't going to compete.' We agreed.

"When we arrived I was so tired, so ill, and so constipated, I thought I'd die. My brother Bill and I had been going down to Ensenada for quite a long time and people knew us there including several maitre 'd's at the restaurants and hotels. I told Bobby my problem and he went out and bought two cans of prune juice. I drank one. Then we were both tired so we rented two rooms and immediately went to sleep. When we awakened it was almost ten p.m. We were hungry but I assured Bobby that even though it was late, 'I know a lovely place where we can eat dinner.' What I'd forgotten was that they served dinner early in the day, and closed the kitchen soon after.

"We went into a place close to the hotel and I introduced Bobby as an artist. It seemed a sin to come to Mexico with him and not have a piano for him to play. But while the restaurant had music

141

from a jukebox, it had no piano. My friend, who owned the bar and restaurant, apologized.

"'We'll go up to the corner where there is another nightclub and see if they have any food,' I said to Bobby. Unfortunately, the club only served drinks, but it did have a piano. As Bobby started playing I glanced out the window and coming down the street were ten or more waiters each carrying an aluminum tray. 'What's going on?' I asked my friend who had accompanied us from his place to the nightclub. 'Oh, I ordered dinner for you and Bobby,' he said. Bobby played and sang as only he could and we had a feast."

* * * * * * * * * * * *
PAUL ROBESON

Few people could be considered as role models for Frances, however, three come readily to mind. One was Dr. Mary McCloud Bethune, another was Margaret Barnes, and the third was Paul Robeson. Frances admired Dr. Bethune for all the work she had done in building her school and in educating the young.

Langston Hughes who had visited Dr. Bethune's school came back and told young Frances and others at Karamu House stories of Bethune's struggle for food and housing for her young students. Dr. Bethune would write to wealthy people all over the country for contributions. Hughes told them about the very wealthy man to whom Dr. Bethune had written to get money for her school to help train these deprived young people. The man reached deeply into his pockets and came up with five dollars and sent it to her. She wrote and thanked him. Others might have been discouraged, but not Dr. Bethune. With that five dollars she bought seeds, planted them, and made money from the crops.

Mary McCloud Bethune had such beautiful speech that whenever Frances would go to hear her speak, she'd write her words down phonetically because Frances hoped a time would come when she could play Dr. Bethune on the stage. Unfortunately, it never happened.

Margaret Barnes and her husband lived in Oberlin with their two sons and a daughter. The oldest son played football and became football coach for Howard University. Margaret Barnes's husband was chef at the college and she was a laundress. She had a professional laundry in which she took care of all the linen for the dormitories at the college. At that time, Shirley Graham, who was then attending Oberlin College, was her secretary. Graham later married W. E. B. DuBois.

"One day, I came into the laundry room which was in the basement and Shirley Graham was sitting on a stool. Margaret Barnes who must have weighed over 300 pounds, big, black, and a wonderful woman, was on the board of the National Council of Negro Women. It was because of Margaret Barnes that I was appointed head of drama for the state of Ohio for three years.

"As she rubbed up and down on a wooden wash board, Margaret Barnes dictated a letter to President Roosevelt, 'Dear Mr. President, I want you to do something about them Scottsboro boys. They're all innocent boys and I want you to do something about them, Mr. President.' What impressed me so was that these wonderful women took time out to do such important things. To be in their presence was inspiring. Mrs. Barnes was a great woman. I always wanted to play her on the stage. Both she and Mary McCloud Bethune deserve to be immortalized."

It seemed to Frances that she'd known Paul Robeson all her life. Actually she first met him when he lectured at Karamu House. He was one of the people she most admired. What she learned from him, she said, would fill volumes. "A powerful man with such charisma and such conviction, Paul's thinking was crystal clear. He had the ability to clarify and relate for you in a way no one else could."

While she was in the Soviet Union, she met John Goode, Essie Robeson's brother, and they both wrote letters to Robeson and his wife urging them to come. Finally in 1935, they did. However, it wasn't until Frances became actively involved with progressive activities that her friendship with Robeson ripened.

In September, 1949, the Progressive Party asked her to be

chairwoman of a rally for Paul Robeson. "This was the first event after Peekskill where Paul was almost killed. They said it would be better if a black woman organized the rally. I readily accepted."

The event was sponsored by *The California Eagle*, published by Charlotta Bass. Bass donated her entire paper to publicize it. Before she switched to the Progressive Party, Bass was the first woman to run for Vice President of the U.S. on the Republican ticket. A member of the Republican Party for thirty years, Bass left when she became convinced that the Party she hailed as Lincoln's Party had become "so far removed in letter and spirit from its   founding" philosophy. In 1950 she ran for Congress from the 14th Congressional District on the Independent Progressive Party ticket.

The rally was to be held at Ridgeley Field, a baseball park at 43rd and Vernon. For several weeks, the organizers held meetings at Frances's house. In each room a group worked on different aspects of the event. Bill Taylor, Chairperson of the Communist Party of Southern California, played a very important role in helping to bring everything together. They received many contributions, however, Frances stipulated that she wouldn't accept contributions unless the contributor knew what the rally stood for. So whenever any one wanted to contribute, she would sit them down and explain the purpose for the rally and exactly what their contributions would be used for.

As a result of so much planning, the rally was a huge success. To prevent the same type of disruption that happened at Peekskill, guards were everywhere. Paul Robeson spoke along with others, choirs sang. Over 1500 people attended. Thousands couldn't get in.

18

ACTIVISM

On October 27, 1951, the National Negro Labor Council (NNLC) held their first convention in Cincinnati. Among the unions represented were delegates from the United Electrical, Radio, and Machine Workers; the United Packinghouse Workers; the Food, Tobacco, Agricultural, and Allied Workers Union; the International Mine, Mill, and Smelter Workers; and the International Fur and Leather Workers. As a trade unionist, Frances was on the board of the NNLC.

Frances's brother Bill lived in Cincinnati. He managed the restaurant and bowling alley that P.L. had purchased. Frances took Paul Robeson and several people as house guests there. "One night we were sitting around talking. The police department had assigned Black policemen to work with us. Paul noticed that whenever this Black policeman who was in charge had to make a decision, he called downtown to see what decision he should make.

"Paul took him aside and said, 'Look sir, I don't want to interfere, but if you are an authority, why aren't you really an authority? This way they're just using you.' Paul explained to him the process of how they had to fight for their own dignity, and if they were supposed to accept responsibility, they should be allowed to accept it and do it fully.

"I'll never forget that whole evening they spent talking back and forth to educate. There were three Black policemen with us. Everywhere Paul went, he taught. Few people know the degree to which he accepted the responsibility to teach and guide and open up thoughts for paths and directions people could go.

"At that conference we learned that the government was threatening to take away Paul's passport which upset me greatly. During a rally, I got up and made a speech. (I must have been nuts.) I said, 'That's alright. They can take it, but Baby, we can do like they did in China to build that wall. They built it handing material from man to man. We can lock our arms and make a bridge across to Europe so that he can walk across our backs and go anywhere he wants to go.'

"I could just see Paul stepping from back to back all the way to Europe. When Paul got up to speak, he said, 'That Frances. She thinks I can do anything.' The conference in Cincinnati was extremely successful."

Eventually, the NNLC was labeled "subversive" and "Communist-dominated" and "a tool of the Soviet Union." (*Organized Labor and the Black Worker*, 1619-1981 by Philip S. Foner pg. 301) and was investigated by the House Committee on Un-American Activities (HUAC). Before its demise, the NNLC was able to win jobs for blacks in several industries, including in the huge department-store chain of Sears-Roebuck, despite the attacks. In 1991, they held a reunion, the first in 40 years. Frances, age 86, despite her ailments and the fact that she needed a wheel chair and a walker, traveled to the reunion alone.

* * * * * * * * * * *

"It was in the thick of the McCarthy period and as a result of all the pressure, Paul had curtailed his outside activities; he had been so mistreated. Because of the harassment put on him, his passport taken away, he had not been in public. Old friends had distanced themselves from him, not wanting others to know of their friendship. Paul came out to the West Coast. Leonytne Price was opening in "Aida" at the opera and I'd gotten tickets and invited him as her guest.

"Later he told me that someone called and said, 'I hear you're going to the opera with Frances. Well, you know Frances dresses. So you can't go in any old blue suit.'

"Paul called and asked if I was going to be dressed. 'Why, of course,' I said. Though I hadn't thought about it at all, I knew something was up when Paul said, 'When Essie and I go to the opera in New York, I just put on my blue suit and we sit in the first balcony.' 'We've got orchestra seats,' I said.

"Paul showed up at my house in a tuxedo looking quite handsome. And he brought his voice with him. He had not been in public because of all the harassment. It was a very rough period. He hadn't been with this group of people before; they were not progressives. When we arrived at the theater, several wealthy women came over and started fluttering around him. He introduced me. Two or three of them came up and invited him to an opening night party after the opera and wanted both of us as their guests. I was so proud.

"After the performance, we went backstage to see Leontyne. When she saw Paul, she practically cried. She said, 'Nothing could have been more important to me. If it hadn't been for Paul, I wouldn't be where I am today. He gave concerts to raise money for me to pay tuition to study.' For two weeks he knew we were going to this concert and not once did Paul mention that he knew her; that he had given concerts to raise money for her training. This was the kind of man he was."

* * * * * * * * * * *

Though Frances had always worked several jobs at the same time, there were times in her life when she was practically penniless. For example, at the time of the rally for Robeson, she had a quarter. Her house had been in foreclosure three times that year, her hot water heater had gone out, and she was in bad shape. "I was a black woman living alone, but I always kept a quarter.

"One time, Paul and I were invited to Jack and Sue Lawson's house for dinner one evening. We were eating when something came up about the Hollywood Writers' Guild.

"Jack said proudly, 'Did you know I was the founder of the Guild?'

"'You were not!' I was shocked. 'That's impossible because no Blacks can get in it.'

"I remembered that when my friend Countee Cullen came out to Hollywood, where he had visited the Hollywood Writers' Guild, and met many of the scriptwriters, some of whom he'd gone to school with. In fact, one of the head writers in the Guild said that he'd never met a more knowledgeable man in his field or more qualified as a writer as Countee Cullen. They were no match for him. Yet, because he was Black, Countee was not allowed to be a member of the Writers' Guild and therefore could not write for Hollywood.

"I was so mad especially because these writers were supposed to be the most progressive people. If their attitude was like this, what the hell could you expect from others? It was a difficult pill to swallow.

"Paul touched my knee and whispered, 'That's alright, baby. We'll talk about it after dinner.' I couldn't conceive anyone like Jack being one of the founders of the Hollywood Writers' Guild. There was not a more prejudiced union in the whole country.

"Jack taught me a wonderful lesson. A couple of years after that evening, he invited me to his home for breakfast. During the interval, Jack had been arrested as one of the Hollywood Ten and had served time in jail. Both he and his wife Sue had eaten at my home a few times, and Sue was very fond of a dish I'd made and asked me for the recipe.

"At his home for brunch one Sunday morning were writers from all over Europe. Because of the many horrible things he and Sue had suffered, she had begun to drink. That day she was high and almost incoherent. Even though all these important people were there, Jack's stature rose over this. He never apologized for his wife's behavior. He simply ignored it and assumed, as he should have been able to, that the people who were there knew why she was in that state and that she deserved the right to be what she was. No one had the right to criticize her. I thought it was the greatest kind of lesson.

"Jack wanted very much to write a play about Paul, but Paul was bigger than life so it was difficult to even contemplate who and what he was. Jack worked on it for years until finally, he got a play together and asked me to read it. Not only did I read it, but I also helped cast it. Then I read it with Bernie Hamilton. I believe we did a very good job.

"The play was never produced because I think the writer was too limited. You could do sections of Paul's life or scenes from the plays he'd done in Europe, but to realistically capture the essence of Paul, I believe, is extremely difficult. Almost fifty years later, I saw Avery Brooks perform as Paul Robeson in a one-man show. He came closer to capturing Paul than anything I have ever seen.

"When Jack died, his son called and asked me to speak at his memorial. For a moment I hesitated. I thought, 'this is a hell of a spot to be in.' All I could think of was the responsibilities he had not met, yet I knew he was a good man. I couldn't think of what to talk about until I remembered what Langston had written on the writers' conference. It went something like this 'The moon and the stars and the trees are all beautiful, but my responsibility is to expose the needs of my people.'"

19

TVA AND EARLY TELEVISION

Frances called the meeting to order. Around the table sat people from the entertainment community, each representing his or her union, two members each from Chorus Equity, the American Guild of Variety Artists, the American Guild of Musical Artists, and Actors' Equity. Along with Frances, Erin O'Brian Moore represented Actors' Equity.

Monday was a good day for the day long meeting. The weather was mild and several items were on the table to be discussed.

"I'd like to take a vote on the proposal from last week," Frances began. "10% of all jobs in every TV production should be set aside for minorities." As she spoke she was aware of the tension in the room that had moments ago been friendly and comfortable. "We can't postpone this any longer." Those sitting closest to her shifted their eyes, avoiding hers. Someone laughed nervously. Erin Moore, sitting across from Frances, nodded in agreement.

"Don't you think we should wait until the chairman arrives?" someone asked.

"Frances was appointed the temporary chair until he comes," Erin Moore responded. "You know because of a conflict in his schedule, he can't make it until the afternoon."

Frances was prepared for a fight. She had been hammering away for the 10% set aside ever since she got on the board. She was determined to succeed. She knew she had several members on her side, maybe enough to carry, she was not sure.

"I think there are matters of more importance to be discussed.

151

We can talk about set asides later," someone else suggested.

The discussion shifted to other issues and continued on into the afternoon. With television gaining in popularity, the union had stepped up its efforts nationwide to have representation in the new industry. The political atmosphere was already charged because of the cold war between the U.S. and the Soviet Union. It was no less charged within the TVA. The problem was not just a matter of gaining recognition and representation, but it was an ideological battle. In an atmosphere of distrust and accusations, the battle between conservatives and progressives, or Left versus Right ideology made accomplishing anything very difficult.

Promptly at one the door opened and in strode the chairman. On seeing Frances in his chair, he threw an astonished look at her and waited until she moved. She knew he disliked her as much as she disliked him. The fact that she'd been appointed temporary chair during his absence only served to infuriate him more. Even after giving up her seat as temporary chair, she continued to hammer away at the industry's hiring practices.

Despite the antagonism Frances encountered as a member of the board of TVA, some things were accomplished, though her attempt to get 10% of the jobs in every television production set aside for minorities lost by three votes.

One of the events TVA sponsored was a fund raiser for sick actors. The union hired professionals to participate in the fund raiser and paid them for their participation. Though Blacks supported the union, not one Black man was hired to participate in the fund raiser. All the money was being given to whites.

"I was so furious I mentioned it. Actually I did more than mention it. I went to an important meeting in New York where I spoke about it fervently. Being the only black member on the committee, many times, I was used as their conscience.

"After the meeting members of TVA were invited to dinner to discuss what we had experienced. Never having been to this section of town before, I was struck by the architecture of the building. Every floor was lit with candles.

"I was enjoying myself when I noticed among the guests, a man named Kornbloom. He was a lawyer and the head of three performing unions, AGVA, Radio Artists, and Actors' Equity. A very prejudiced man, he hated me because I exposed him.

"When *Cabin in the Sky* came to California, Kornbloom wrote a letter back to New York in which he said that 'a lot of clouds had come to the west coast and it was raining heavily.' He didn't think he should write these people up as members of Actors' Equity. Instead, they should be given some kind of permit to work.

"For many years, I had fussed and fought, until finally Actors' Equity hired a black office worker. This young lady found this letter and gave it to me. That's how I learned of what he had said. He was a horrible man and he knew I knew it. I sat right on him and wouldn't give him an inch.

"After an exquisite dinner at this lovely house, I was talking to a group of people when I saw him going up the wrought iron staircase. I don't know if he had been listening to my conversation and not paying attention to what he was doing because just as he reached the top, he suddenly toppled backwards down the stairs.

"During that time I really wasn't aware of what was happening until someone came to me and said, 'Oh, I see you have two or three pages in the bible.' He explained what the bible was. A man named Gilbert, a communist instigator, had written a pamphlet which became known as 'the bible.' It contained several pages of names of people suspected of being communist or having communist affiliations.

"I first saw Gilbert at a meeting I attended. The purpose of the meeting was to inform people about what was happening in the industry which was under attack from the House Un-American Activities Committee or HUAC.

"Gilbert strode in, took off his coat, but not his hat, and sat down. 'Well, let's get this thing straightened out. Let's tell these damn communists what they are going to do. Let's get going,' he said in a presumptive manner.

"'That's not what I came here for,' I said calmly. I told him what I had come for and promptly left.

"At another time during a televised meeting, we were seated around a coffee table and most of the people present were smoking. Every time Gilbert wanted to say something, I'd interrupt him and say, 'Pardon me, do you have a cigarette?' and he'd reach into his pocket and give me one. Then he'd start again and I'd interrupt him. 'Do you have a light?' I kept interrupting him throwing him completely off."

With the onslaught of the McCarthy Era, Actors' Equity and TVA were under attack. In an attempt at intimidation, some FBI men came out to Frances's house. They wanted her to name friends and acquaintances who were affiliated with progressive causes. She told them she'd give them a list of grievances she had and "when you can meet these, than you can talk to me about something else." They went away and never returned.

"A few months later, I was on the train coming back to Los Angeles, from Minnesota. Seated beside me was a very nice black man. We were enjoying each other's company when I looked up and saw Chris O'Brian, who was the head of Actors' Equity Association, coming down the aisle toward me. He was so shocked to see me, he stopped and said, 'Oh Frances, will you come with me and have a drink and maybe have dinner together?' 'Yes,' I said and excused myself. This black man with whom I was sitting became so insulted that I had gone off with this blue-eyed, curly-headed white man, I could feel the strain. When I returned to my seat, I discovered that he had moved.

"Later, in Hollywood, Chris called me. I was in the process of resigning from the board of TVA, and he called to ask if I wanted him to write my letter of resignation. 'I'm a lawyer and my uncle is the head of ACLU in New York,' he said. 'I would like to write your letter of resignation.' I had been asked to resign from TVA because I was a progressive and because I refused to sign the loyalty oath.

"I thanked him. 'No,' I said. 'I'll do it myself.' At around two o'clock in the morning, I decided that no white man could write my letter for me and say what I wanted to say. I wrote my own letter and when I read it to the TVA committee, everybody cried. I guess I did too."

On June 20, 1952, Frances delivered her resignation speech to the committee. In her speech, Frances related a true incident which later formed the basis of a play entitled "Trial By Fire." Written by a priest, "Trial by Fire" was the story of a Black family who moved into a previously all white area in Fullerton, California. The husband, an army veteran, his wife and daughter were harassed by their white neighbors and their house burned down. It was a moving play.

"Myrtle Pitts's daughter, Phyllis, played the part of the young child. When she first played the role in which she is called a nigger, she didn't know what the term meant. But when she played it again a year or two later, because she knew what a nigger was from their point of view, it made a great deal of difference in her performance. I told them this in my speech, and I added 'We don't need others to play roles meant for other ethnic groups.'"

As a result of that speech, Frances was able to get more parts for ethnic actors. Though it was mostly as extras, it wasn't likely that the industry would have thought of giving them to Blacks before. Frances had been in TVA from the beginning and had been involved in the last convention that preceded the formation of the American Federation of Television and Radio Artists (AFTRA.)

"Though it was a struggle, it was really a growing experience for me. I paid quite a price, but at the time I was so busy trying to correct what I saw as injustices that I wasn't aware of the cost until much later. "

Prior to this, Frances' film career was constant. After her resignation from TVA, a year would pass before she worked in film again.

* * * * * * * * * * *

ERIN O'BRIAN MOORE AND KATE DRAIN LAWSON

"Among the people on the board of TVA I counted as friends

was Erin O'Brian Moore. Erin and her mother lived in Los Angeles. Erin had been in a terrible fire that required her to have to sleep on thirty-two small pillows. However, she recovered. At that time Erin was going with a reactionary southern senator.

"I don't know why Erin and her mother had such a warm feeling about me, but once her mother came to me and said, 'There're not many things I can do, and I don't have the know-how to do it that you have. I know that it takes a lot of money to keep yourself groomed, but I want you to know that I want to give you a certain amount each week.' From time to time she would give me money.

When I went to the meeting in New York, Erin's mother who had a very good mink coat wrote to her furrier giving me permission to wear that coat while I was there.

"Another member of the TVA board with whom I became very close was Kate Drain Lawson. We went through a lot together. One day, near the end of June, I went to Los Angeles City College to see a production of *Othello* performed by the students in the drama department. In the cast were Paul Winfield and Al Freeman, Jr. After the play, I went backstage to talk to the cast. I asked several of them what they were doing over the summer.

"The white members of the cast all said they would be doing summer stock. When I asked Paul, he shrugged and said he wasn't sure. 'Probably get a job as a janitor or something.' I was quite annoyed.

"Morris Kanopsky was scheduled to come to town to appear in a production of *King Lear*. I called my friend Kate Drain Lawson who was very active in television and also designed costumes for Bob Hope and many television personalities. I told her to tell Morris Kanopsky I wanted Paul in that production. Kate worked hard to see that not only Paul, but other blacks as well were included in the cast."

20

———

SALT OF THE EARTH

During the 1950's, Senator Joseph McCarthy and the House UnAmerican Activities Committee, went on a mission seeking to rid the film industry of anyone who was progressive or left-leaning. The result was many in the industry were blacklisted. Several of the blacklisted members formed a film production company. Among them were Herbert Biberman, Paul Jarrico, Albert Maltz, Michael Wilson, and Adrian Scott.

As their first project, they wanted to make a picture based on a true incident about a woman who loses custody of her children because of her political beliefs. The whole incident became a national scandal. This group of producers, directors, and writers asked a well-known writer, who was then living in Mexico, to write a screen version of this incident.

When several members came to New York, some of the cultural workers- people in the progressive party who worked with the arts- asked them why Frances had not been invited to become a member of their production company. There were not many progressive black people in film and theater on the West Coast. Frances was on the board of Actors' Equity, Actors' Lab, the Circle Theatre, and Cosmos, and she was active in film, having helped to form the black caucus in SAG and having studied with them at the Actors' Lab in Hollywood. Also, she had lectured twice at the Lee Strausberg Studio in New York. Her credentials were impeccable.

At that time she was in the city being interviewed for a play.

157

Somehow they located her and invited her to have dinner with them at a fancy restaurant. It was quite a dinner! Everything was done at the table - meats cooked, salad tossed, desserts prepared. Her gastronomical taste buds were satisfied. During dinner they told her the story and their treatment of it. As she listened, she found that she disagreed with so much of it that rather than say anything, she sat back and enjoyed the dinner. Finally she had to say something. "I don't agree with anything you've told me."

A gasp went around the table. One of them said, "You what!"

"I think it's completely wrong. I don't agree with your treatment," she said. "The film should not be done in this form." They did not convey anything that was believable as she knew life in the U.S. to be.

(Frances's comments written on the inside cover of the script.

"I feel this case is too isolated from the people - It is a peoples (sic) case - audience must understand how important their role of fighting through for full freedom for all people around them is against the wishes of the powers that be because this would give people the strength necessary to prevent wars and exploitation of the people[.] They should understand most of them could be a Catherine if they put just a little more effort in their fight where they are and thus strike a telling blow against war. Help them to identify with [the] heroine.")

"Well, we can't leave it like this. We'll have to finish talking. Do you have time later tonight?" Jarrico asked. She didn't have any particular plans so she said yes. They called a friend of theirs who had an apartment nearby, and they went there to continue the conversation.

At 2:30 in the morning, they were still at an impasse. Seeing that they were getting nowhere, Frances said, "Look, I'm tired. Let me just go downstairs and walk a bit." She took the elevator down to the lobby where she located a public phone and telephoned Paul Robeson. She knew that everyone was awed by Paul Robeson's opinions. Because he had this wonderful ability to really clarify without alienating, his judgement was heeded and respected. You felt you were a better human being for having been exposed to him.

After a few rings, Paul answered. "I hate to disturb you," she apologized, "but I don't know what else to do."

"Don't be sorry, Fran," he said. "You wouldn't call me if you didn't need me. Where are you? I will be there in ten minutes."

Before returning to the apartment, she smoked a cigarette and paced the lobby. Finally, she went up and announced that she had called Paul Robeson, and he was coming over. "We'll talk about it more fully when he gets here." The men were more than a little surprised.

Robeson came right away. After hearing their concept and treatment, he shook his head. He told them that he agreed with everything Frances had said, and before he was through, he made them rethink their attitude about the whole project. Grateful, she reflected, "I'd been alone, a black woman in a room with several of the most learned white men in the industry." After that meeting, they asked her to be a part of their production company.

At that time Carleton Moss, a brilliant, well-respected black writer and film maker had been asked to produce one of their projects; however, he refused. "Carleton knew that he worked best alone, so he created his own documentaries for which he was given a budget. Rather than dissipate his energy needlessly bickering, he had the wisdom to know to what he should give his priorities."

Today, while there are a number of very fine African American directors in Hollywood, in the 1950's there were none. Once Frances asked a producer how she could become a director. She'd always wanted to direct film. "There are several strikes against you," he said in a matter-of-fact tone, "First, you're a woman; second, you're black; and third, I don't know of a producer who would hire you. Besides, most directors come in with their own crew."

"I can't do anything about the first two strikes," she responded, "but if you'll invite me to a cocktail party where the film deals are made, I'll do the rest." Needless to say, she never got an invitation.

Frances accepted the offer made by this group of progressives because, like her decision to enter the Hollywood film community, she believed she could change things. Not until she was asked to work on *Salt of the Earth* did she have the opportunity to be a director.

* *********************************

In the late 1940's members of the Mine Mill Local 890 organized a strike against the Delaware Zinc Company in Silver City, New Mexico, protesting low wages, poor working conditions, minimal safety conditions, and the inadequate and unsanitary facilities in the shacks where the workers had to live.

Clinton Jencks, who was a union representative in Northern New Mexico, told Paul Jarrico about the strike. Jarrico, who at the time was looking for a project to do with his newly formed company, liked the idea, wrote an outline and presented it to the mine workers. Before it received the approval of the workers, it went through sixteen rewrites. At the insistence of Bill Taylor, Frances joined the project while it was still in Los Angeles.

"It was an exciting project and I was looking forward to being a part of it even though at the time I was doing another picture. *Salt of the Earth* was to be filmed on location in New Mexico. We began some of the casting in my home."

In an interview with the author, Carlton Moss said that before they approached Frances, he was asked to be a part the *Salt of the Earth* project. He refused. "How could I explain being a part of a project that had little benefit for or relevancy to the black community?" (Moss interview with the author, Los Angeles, CA. August 20, 1996.)

In the original script, an Anglo couple were supposed to play the lead. However, that was changed. Then, Sonja Dal was hired to play Esperanza Quintero, the lead role. She insisted on having a professional star play opposite her. Bert Corona was hired by the company to search for a Mexican lead to play the role opposite Dal. However, when no one could be found, Sonja Dal dropped out. Rosaura Revueltas, an actress whose family were activists, accepted the part. Juan Chacon, president of Local 890 and a non professional actor, was selected to play Ramon Quintero.

"I insisted on having some black technicians as a part of the production staff; however, we couldn't find any black technicians in Los Angeles. I was able to get a young cameraman named Hillburn who was working with a documentary group in New York to come out and work with us. He was the first black technician hired to work on a picture in Hollywood.

"When the time came to go down to New Mexico, unfortunately, because of my other commitment, I couldn't go along with the crew. As soon as I was free, though, I told them I would come down. Everything went fine until just before the production left for New Mexico.

"At our last meeting in Los Angeles, some of the men questioned whether I should go. My reputation as a fighter was thought to be detrimental to the project. 'You know, Frances,' they said, 'the Mexicans are very different from the Blacks. They're very prejudiced. They don't really accept Blacks. They're very docile and take things in stride. They don't protest the way you and your people do.' In other words, they wanted me to keep quiet.

"I held my peace, thinking of the irony in the situation. 'We're going down to see mine workers who are mostly Mexican Americans and who are on strike! And they don't fight?'

"A few weeks later, with all this caution given me, I went down to New Mexico. Filming hadn't begun as yet. The first thing I noticed with some consternation, was that the group had rented a recreation clubhouse with a screened-in porch, and a spectacular view overlooking the city, a resort kind of place that was used for vacationers when they came to New Mexico. I protested. None of us knew enough about the Spanish language, and we didn't know enough about the people. I felt we should be living with the people in their homes so that we could understand them and what their grievances were. That was the first big fight we had.

"The night before we started production, we called the actors, the chief technicians, and the members of the production

161

company who were in town and had a meeting in the recreation clubhouse lounge. We were all sitting around the fireplace getting acquainted, discussing the project and getting feedback from the people involved especially the actors. Both Rosaura Revueltas, the female lead, and Juan Chacon, the male lead, were there.

"The conversation somehow got around to the militancy of the Mexican people. Once again, Herb and Paul said that Mexicans were docile, not fighting people, as if whatever happened was acceptable. I was very annoyed. Every group of people fight for their own truth and dignity, and to assume that they don't is unbelievable! Finally I had to interrupt. Turning to Revueltas, I said, 'Pardon me. Didn't you folks fight in several revolutions?'

'Of course,' she said. 'We're very militant people.'

'That's what I thought,' I said. 'These people don't seem to understand that. Why don't you explain to them.'

"At first she hesitated, saying it really didn't matter. When I insisted, she said. 'We stand for what is right and we're willing to fight for it.' Someone quickly changed the subject. I think the men were shamed into a position they did not want to face.

"As the assistant director I would get the actors together to go over their lines and set the tempo. I made sure that the people knew what they were doing and why. Because of my role, I was able to build up a rapport with many of the people that I would not otherwise have been able to.

"The next Sunday, the first full day that I was there, some of the mine workers came to me and said, 'Maybe you can help us. These men don't know where we are and their attitude is going to cause those of us who are still working and even the ones on strike who are still on payroll to lose our jobs because they don't understand. Will you speak to them?' I said I would.

"I called a meeting and the production heads were shocked about the whole thing. Mike Wilson said he could understand where I was coming from. But the two main people who were working on the project, Paul Jarrico, the producer and Herb Biberman, the director who had helped with the writing, didn't want the meeting.

But others were in my corner. After receiving pressure from Virginia Jencks, Mike Wilson, and Adrian Scott, Biberman and Jarrico gave in.

"For a while everything ran smoothly; then one day, the Mexican workers came to me again and said, 'Look, these people are really going to ruin things for us.' Incensed and unhappy, they told me that the company had advertised on the radio for extras on this picture which was supposed to be sub rosa. The workers knew how to reach the people we needed, they reasoned. By not respecting their opinions, the producers had insulted them.

"Equally infuriated, I called another meeting, but the production heads didn't want to come. I located Mike Wilson and Adrian Scott and explained what was happening with the trade union members. Mike and Adrian were the only two men I respected from that group. Mike agreed with me that we should have a meeting. Together with Virginia Jencks and Mike Wilson, we went to see Paul Jarrico.

'We're going to have a meeting today,' I said. However, he was not interested. 'We don't have time,' he responded.

'Dammit!' I shouted pounding my fist on his desk, 'We'll take time!'

"We had the meeting. Despite the fact that we got a number of things straightened out, these foolish men went back to their technique of trying to hire people over the radio. It was disastrous; We almost lost the whole project.

"The next day, Paul and Herb were coming up the steps, and as they passed my bedroom which was located at the head of the stairs, I could hear them talking. Herb said he hadn't slept a wink all night because 'that woman (meaning me) was driving him crazy.' He didn't know what he was going to do, he said. Paul agreed. I thought to myself, 'Man, you ain't heard nothing yet.'

"I knew about Herb Biberman before working with him on *Salt of the Earth* . A few years earlier, Herb wrote a screenplay called *New Orleans* . He went to New York to get Billy Holiday to play one of the important parts in the picture, but Billy didn't want to be in pictures yet, she told me, because 'I didn't like the way films depicted my people.'

'But it's a beautiful part and it's written for you. You just have to do it,' Biberman had responded. 'It'll be a wonderful way for you to display your talent.'

'Well, I'll have to think about it,' Billy said.

"And she did think about it. Herb went back to New York two or three times, and finally he came back with a contract that was so attractive and with a salary that was too tempting to pass up. He explained again that it was a special part written for her and that she should do it. Finally, even without reading the script, she agreed to do it.

"I had gotten to know Billy when she was singing in a nightclub on Western Avenue. The public relations people I was working with took me down to this club to take publicity pictures with her. When she came out to California to do the film, *New Orleans,* we spent some time together. Afterwards she told me 'Do you know what that so and so did, Frances? He wrote my part so that I was just a glorified kitchen maid. I have worked all my life singing in nightclubs and dumps so that I wouldn't have to be somebody's servant or cook and that's all that part was about. I was so disgusted.'

"I was not surprised when I discovered that some of the production staff were limited in their outlook. Nonetheless, I felt that I'd played an important role while I was there. However because I had been working on a picture in Hollywood, I had to leave before *Salt of the Earth* was completed."

The film realistically portrayed the real-life struggle of striking zinc mine workers fighting for equality in all areas. With their wives and family support, the striking mine workers are successful. *Salt...* was groundbreaking in that it dealt with areas previously taboo for Hollywood - the plight of Hispanic workers, and equality for women. It included non professional actors, many of whom were actual zinc mine workers. Had Frances not been there, according to Lorenzo Torrez, who appeared in the film and who played himself, one of the striking mine workers, the role of the miners would have been minute. In a telephone interview with the author, 6 October, 1996, Torrez said, Frances encouraged them to talk about their feelings and the problems they encountered during filming. While the filmmakers included Frances on their project, "she was never really accepted."

Throughout the production both internal and external conflicts threatened to kill the project. Corporate heads tried to stop production, the actors and technicians were harassed. An article in *The World*, May 1, 1976, cites some of the outside forces at work to halt the making and showing of the film.

> "Pathe Lab would not permit film processing during production making it impossible for the crew to watch the daily rushes. Sound recordings were ruined by planes that were sent to fly low over shooting locations. In Congress, Representative Donald Jackson warned the film would destroy U.S. credibility in Latin America. Victor Riesel, reactionary columnist, accused the people working on the film of providing cover for enemy agents to infiltrate and collect data on nuclear weapons research at Los Alamos....film projectionists were warned by their union against showing the film... and Immigration and Naturalization Service deported Rosaura Revueltas on a phony charge of not having her visa properly stamped."

While the film makers have been honored for their artistic achievement, little recognition has been given to the mine workers. As a result of the strike, while not all their problems were resolved, they did achieve a contract based on the Fair Employment Practices Commission. The problem of housing was resolved when the company, realizing the segregated housing was no longer profitable, sold its housing to the city and private companies who renovated them and gave the workers the option to purchase their homes.

In addition, companies were no longer allowed to use the courts or the sheriff's department to break strikes as was a common practice prior to the strike. As a result of the film's focussing the attention on the plight of the mine workers, the workers were able to gain participation on the executive board. Finally, the film helped to garner public support for the trade union movements throughout the south and southwest.

Some of the repercussions were that companies fought even harder to destroy the union. With FBI help, trade union members were constantly harassed, files were compiled, individuals were followed and intimidated. As a result, many union leaders left the area, and some quieted their activities. (Torrez, telephone conversation.)

"Despite the problems, *Salt of the Earth* was a good picture with good actors; I'd helped to cast it. I'd gotten actors like Will Geer and David Wolfe. Working on the film used a lot of energy from me and I'm sure from the others as well. I think I paid a terrific price. Up until that time I had been working steadily and building up a good reputation. It was at least five years before I got another film role.

"Toward the end of the picture, Adrian Scott said to me, 'Frances, you really need to rest.'

'When I finish the picture, I'll do that.'

'Tell you what,' he said. 'I go to a psychiatrist several times a week. If I arrange for you to go see one, will you go? It cost thirty dollars a session, but I'll pay for one session a week, if you'll go.'

'Adrian, I really appreciate that,' I said. 'I know you're concerned, and I love the way you express it. But let me tell you the difference between you and me. You're going to the psychiatrist because you don't know what's the matter with you. I know what's the matter with me and when I get through here, I'll do something about it.'

"One of the things I did when I came home was to purchase a big house on the corner of Arlington and Adams. I bought that house for eleven thousand dollars at that time. It had to be completely renovated. I stripped off the wallpaper, refinished the woodwork, painted everything, laid all the linoleum in the kitchen and baths and did the whole house over myself. For me, that was therapeutic.

"When I finished, I was all right. I'd gotten the ugly part of *Salt of the Earth* out of my system. The irony is that even with their lack of respect for other people's dignity, it was a landmark picture. It was a workers' picture and because I was closer to the workers' plight, it was easier for me to understand their struggle and fight with them."

21

LIVE AT THE 5-4 BALLROOM

For two years from 1955 to 1957, Pete Morgan and I probably had the first live television show from Los Angeles. We had a 90 minute TV show at KCOP, Channel 13. Pete and I were co-producers. I was also the director and choreographer. Pete was in construction. In addition to Pete and myself, the production staff included John Moreland, James Edwards, and a number of others.

"John Moreland was an excellent writer but an arrogant s.o.b. who sometimes embarrassed me with the writing of Black or Jewish people or any ethnic dialogue. A staunch Republican, John used to write political speeches for Nixon and Reagan and many presidential candidates. He worshipped his mother and being her last child, she worshipped him. His father, a hardworking man, owned a marshmallow factory where he made John work sometimes. I admired his mother and father a great deal.

"John loved to write sonnets and plays that were so long they had to be cut in half to be produced. He loved to use unusual polysyllabic words. I first met John at Duke Ellington's production of 'Jump for Joy.' He and I had great rapport.

"James Edwards, a fine young actor, M.C.'d all our shows. He had been in the army and had been wounded which resulted in his having a steel plate in his head. Always youthful looking, his face had been reconstructed so that it didn't change whether he was happy or in pain.

"Much of the planning for the show was done either at my house or at John's. Unfortunately, John, my arrogant writer friend

167

and Jimmy Edwards who was also a brilliant, well-read man were antagonistic towards each other. Always at each other's throat, they could never get along. Many times the meetings would last until 2 a.m. More than a few times, I stood in the driveway between a knife, John and Jimmy. It's a wonder I didn't get cut.

"The show was ninety minutes long, with the first fifteen minutes spent on the life of an important artist such as Fats Waller, Mamie Smith, or Billy Holiday, and the second fifteen minutes a dramatization of a significant part of their lives. Usually in the dramatic part, I portrayed the mother or aunt. The last hour of the show was musical. We included the music the person was known for and had someone who knew the artist talk about that person.

"We had on the show a colleague of Fats Waller. His music was so much like Fats' you couldn't discern the difference. He told anecdotes about Fats who was always in debt. The collectors would come into the theater, wait for the intermission or the end of Fats's performance, and then try to nab him to get the money due them. However, Fats was always ready for them. He would have this man who looked so much like him replace him during intermission and the man would do the last half of the program. When the lights came on, all the people with whom Fats was indebted would be shocked to discover that Fats had slipped away.

"Fats was known for his house rent parties. At that time in Harlem people had little money; the rents were very high. To get the money for the rent, they'd give house rent parties where they'd sell food like pigs' feet, or pigs' tail, salad, beans and rice, very solid food. Usually on Saturday night Fats would play the piano while the people danced or played cards until early morning.

"We found much talent at that time. We found a woman who looked just like Joan Crawford. Sometimes we'd try to get well known people to portray other celebrities. Once we wanted to get Dinah Washington to do the Bessie Smith role. At that time she was working in a club downtown and going with a very handsome, light-skinned man who was charming and sophisticated. She was not.

"When I visited the club where she was performing, her

boyfriend invited me to their table to wait for Dinah. I sat down and had a drink. When she came, she attacked me, called me names, said she wouldn't work for me or anyone like me, and then she pulled out a knife and threatened to cut my throat. Needless to say she didn't work on our show though I would have signed her anyway because she was a great blues singer.

"At that time, we were the only all-black production company that did live shows on television. The show aired Sundays at 5 p.m. at the 5-4 Ballroom at Broadway and 54th Street.

"Every week we had to look for Jimmy. As a hedge, I would try to keep up with him on Saturday nights so we could find him on Sunday mornings for a full rehearsal before we went on.

"A young friend of my brother P.L.'s came out from Cincinnati. P.L. owned a restaurant bar and bowling alley which Brother Bill managed. When this man came out here, Bill told him to look me up which he did, and we gave him a job. One of this man's chores was to go out and locate Jimmy, find out where he was, so we could send someone out to bring him back bodily.

"One day, Jimmy was ready when the man came looking for him. When the doorbell rang, he had his blond friend open the door for this black man who had just come from Cincinnati which is like living in the deep South. Completely nude, she welcomed him very formally and told him to have a seat. Jimmy sent her back out with a feather duster and told her to dust the whole room while the man waited for him to get dressed. This was Jimmy's idea of a good joke.

"Another time we had Odetta on the show. At that time she drove an ugly black touring car. A large black woman with great authority, Odetta was driving on Hollywood Blvd. when she saw Jimmy Edwards driving in another car with two or three blond women. She forced them to the side and made them park. Then she made Jimmy get out of his car and into hers. He was too weak from laughing to do anything to stop her.

"Getting that production together was no simple task. We had actors, the people who imitated the artists' voices and eight to ten dancers. Many times I had to choreograph and even join in the

169

dance numbers. All together, they were good shows because John was a good writer and I wasn't the worst director. It became a very popular thing to do on Sunday afternoons in L.A.

"I was the only woman in that production staff; I had to be mother, father, aunt, uncle, and nurse. If there was a job that needed to be done, I had to do it. But I was used to working that way even in theater. In fact, it was the way I was trained to work. Eventually, we ran out of money and the show was cancelled."

* * * * * * * * * * *

"Langston Hughes wrote a book called *Sweet Fly Paper of Life*, charming story with a blues section in it. I was performing in it on Sunset Strip with a young man named Bumps Blackwell who was probably one of the best mixers of sound. We did an entire production at the Ash Grove on Sunset Blvd., and later we did it for two years in Las Vegas. It starred Bessie Griffin and the Gospel Pearls with Eddie Kendricks. It was so successful that Langston came out from New York to see it." According to Ed Pearle, owner of the Ash Grove, Sweet Fly Paper of Life was the introduction of gospel into the 'broader community.' "It gave me the connection to the religious community of So. Central." (Telephone interview with the author, July, 1996)

"My friend Phil Carey Jones was on the executive board of Actors' Equity. Phil met Maya Angelou somewhere in Hollywood and one evening, he went up to her and said, 'You must know Frances Williams.' Maya said, 'I don't believe I do.' Phil insisted that she meet me. He called me and told me. I invited them over for dinner on Sunday. I fixed an Italian veal dish. Soon Phil came. 'Didn't you bring the lady?' I asked. 'As I drove up, I saw her sitting out front in her car,' he answered. He went out and brought her in and that's how we met. We had a great evening.

"At that time I was working for a construction company on Western and 29th Street. I had to be at work at 6 a.m. to get the men started. After that I worked in Hollywood with Bumps on his project until two a.m. One evening, Maya came by just as I was finishing up the production. 'I've got to talk with you,' she said. I told her my schedule.

"Maya sang the blues very well, and I've always had the belief that to sing the blues effectively, you had to have had the experience to know what you were singing about to impart it so that it had any affect on people. I couldn't understand how such a young woman could   comprehend this so well.

"That night Maya came into my dressingroom on the Strip and talked, and talked. We talked until about five forty-five in the morning. Then I had to rush off to work at the construction site. Later we continued. During that period, I probably learned everything she wrote in *I Know Why the Caged Bird Sings.* I was really devastated.

'Now I know why you can sing the blues and make it believable,' I said. She'd been through so much.

"We became very good friends. When Maya returned from Ghana, she and her son Guy came here to live. During the winter she got a job in New York. Coincidentally, a friend who was a costume designer telephoned me and said she would be moving to the West Coast. 'I'm so tall. I have all these coats and suits that I'd like someone to use.' They were just right for Maya. I got them together.

"At almost the same time Maya came to live in one of the front apartments, Beah Richards came to live in the other. We called it 'the Compound.' Beah came up from Mississippi. She had been at the Globe theatre in San Diego, and had written a play. Someone told her to see me.

"I was stage manager of a theater production in Hollywood. This little woman came with her script and sat on my porch. I told her I didn't know how I could see her because my schedule was so tight. I had to run to Hollywood to get the theater set up and that went on until midnight. I told her, 'I don't know how I am going to get time for you.'

"Finally, I decided to take the script and read it between scenes. It was a mind blower. I liked it! We became very close after that."

22

___

A RAISIN IN THE SUN

One of the few people in California who knew my mother was Louise Brooks. Because she knew my mother, Louise felt responsible for me even though I was a grown woman. Almost every day she would call me up and keep me on the phone for hours, scolding me for smoking; I smoked cigarettes quite heavily then. If she'd see me with a glass of wine, she'd scold me about that. Her conversations went on so long that many times I couldn't get anything done. No excuse I could come up with would end the conversation. Finally, I'd put the phone down, complete whatever I had to do, come back to the phone every once in a while and grunt. This satisfied her, and I was able to accomplish things.

"Phil Selznick, who later became an executive at Warner Brothers, brought Louise out to Los Angeles and set her up in business. She opened a seafood restaurant on the Sunset Strip, the first African American business woman on that street. To her customers, she was Mammy Louise. But to others, she would say, 'My name is Louise Brooks. Some people call me Mammy Louise, but that's business!'

"I was in her restaurant the day a man came in with his friend. 'You remember Mammy Louise from Cleveland?' he said introducing her to his friend. 'She was the best bootlegger in Cleveland.'

"Louise just laughed. She told me she used to make liquor during Prohibition, cases and cases of liquor before she was caught and brought before the judge. On the day of the trial, she brought the judge two of her lemon meringue pies and won the case.

"Louise and her brother Maurice were found by the Salvation Army in the doorway of a building in Cleveland. Later, she married a man named Undergrove and both worked as janitors of an apartment across from where we lived. When I was six years old, Brooksy, as we called her, taught me to toe dance.

"Louise became a famous cook. No one could make a lemon pie or cook seafood like she could. I had been in Los Angeles for a few years before I ran into Louise at the Dunbar Hotel, a very attractive hotel, at 41st Street and Central Ave where big bands like Duke Ellington played in their auditorium. She had taken over the restaurant there and she served excellent food.

"Once she became very ill, and with no one to take over the restaurant for her, I told her I would do it. To my dismay, I found that waitresses she trusted were stealing money. When I told her about it she didn't believe me. 'Oh no, they couldn't have,' she said, so I had to prove it. I'd always wanted to have a restaurant of my own, but after six months of managing hers, I was cured.

"Louise taught me a lot about politics. When she was seventy, she organized one hundred black women into the Mary McCloud Bethune Party, a wing of the Democratic Party. What I learned from her was very useful when Frederick O'Neal ran for president of Actors' Equity."

* * * * * * * * * * *

"Frederick O' Neal was one of the first African Americans to play roles other than manservant, chauffeur, or cook in a Broadway play. Though he played a variety of roles, his claim to fame was his role as a detective. Fred was one of the officers at the National Actors Equity Association in New York. Because of his influence, I got on the board of Actors' Equity Association.

"In the early fifties, Ralph Bellamy who had been president of Actors' Equity for many years, decided he wasn't going to run for another term. A member of the board, Fred O'Neal went to him and said, 'Ralph, are you sure you aren't going to run?' Ralph said no, that he'd had enough. Fred decided he'd throw his hat in the ring. When it became known that Fred was going to run for that office, Bellamy's white cohorts went to him and said, 'You can't let that black man become president. You've got to run again.'

"When I heard about this, I got very angry as did many others in Actors' Equity. We decided to support Fred's bid for president. I headed the campaign on the west coast. And a man named Wellington headed it on the east coast. It was an uphill battle because no Negro had ever been national president of a trade union in this country before.

"On the executive board of Actors' Equity in California was a lawyer whom everyone respected. I was grateful when he came out in support of my efforts. When we were having a rally for Fred, he spoke before the audience. 'Now I've worked with Frances Williams a long time and I don't always agree with everything Miss Williams says, but I have never seen her shove anything under the rug. If she tells you something, you might just as well believe it.'

"My final thrust on getting Fred elected was based on a story I heard from Mammy Louise Brooks. We had almost no black political officials in California at the time when she started her group of one hundred Black women. Her Mary McCloud Bethune wing of the Democratic Party was so effective registering and getting blacks out to vote, that for the first time, the Democratic party decided to let them nominate an African American to run for city office.

"The women put together a list of several African Americans. From the list they had to choose one to run. However, because they knew them all so intimately, all the little petty things came up, and they couldn't decide who to select. After a long debate that seemed to be leading nowhere, Louise Brooks who was president of the organization stepped up. She said, 'Alright, so we've got some black sons-of-bitches. We've had a hell of a lot of white ones for a long time.'

"I used this story in my speech for Fred O'Neal. I said, 'Look, the man is qualified. He's had business experience, and he's been exposed to all our problems in Actors' Equity. Even if he is a son-of-a-bitch, we've had a hell of a lot of white ones. So let's elect a man who knows our needs and can do the job.' Fred won the election and became the first black man to head a national trade union.

"I served on the board of Actors' Equity for about twenty years until I resigned to go to Mexico. While I was on the board, I helped set up the minority committee on work codes. I worked on the Ethnic Minority Committee, the House Ways and Means Committee, and the Legislative Committee. We had workshops at my house to teach blacks in the industry how to fight for better jobs, what questions to ask. Many blacks who were working in the industry and those unemployed came, but there were some who came to break up the Caucus. When I left, I recommended Virginia Capers to take my place but they said she was too much like me.

"When Ronald Reagan became president of SAG, he abolished the Black Caucus. It was reestablished years later under the leadership of Robert Doqui. The Minority Committee at SAG, a committee I helped set up with a number of young people, was dissolved by Ronald Reagan without telling us. Celena Royal and others got it reinstated."

* * * * * * * * * * *

"Once I went on a cruise with Ernest Holmes, founder of the Church of Religious Science in Los Angeles. Holmes told everyone to take out the smallest coin they had. Everyone took out a penny and held it in their hand. Next he said take out the biggest coin you have. Some took out quarters, others took out dimes. I had nothing. I said I have the entire horizon. Ernest said to me, 'You'll never be a millionaire, but you'll never want for money.'

"I was taking a course taught by this wonderful man who interpreted dreams and helped you cope with them. He had rented rooms in a beautiful hotel that was situated on a mountain peak somewhere outside the city.

"One day in class, I told him about a dream I had had. I said, 'I was in this little town with all these houses - blue, yellow, purple, pink, all different colors, and the sun was shining. It was beautiful.' I also told him I was doing my whole house over, especially the kitchen. At that time I had decided to do my kitchen over - I planned to change the cupboards, redo the floors, and paint the walls.

'That's interesting,' he said, 'but I don't know how you're going to finish it because in two weeks, you'll be in New York.' In two weeks I was in New York, on Broadway doing the play, *A Raisin in the Sun*, replacing Claudia McNeil who went to Hollywood to do the film version. The play ran there for two years.

"After Broadway, *A Raisin in the Sun* went on tour. One of our first stops was in Chicago. While I was there, I visited the Church of Religious Science. I was already a practitioner when I went to Chicago, and for some reason, I was very inspired and clear there. Someone told me that beneath the city the composition of the earth does something physically to the area."

* * * * * * * * * * *

FANNIE LOU HAMER

"While I was doing *A Raisin in the Sun*, Fannie Lou Hamer came to Chicago for two weeks, and I secured a ticket for her. She had never seen a play before, let alone a play with black actors. She was touched, and I was very glad because this gave me an opportunity to get to know her better and to learn more about the struggle to get the vote in Mississippi. We saw each other almost daily until she left Chicago.

"She told me two stories about the struggle to get the vote. The owners of the shacks wanted to evict the tenants who were fighting to get the vote. 'The roofs we had, if you came by in the morning and said 'Good mornin', Miss Hamer,' you wouldn't have to go to the door. You'd just reach your hand through the ceiling and shake hands, and say 'Good mornin, Sister Jones.'

"Another story she told me that was quite delightful. The farmers raised hogs and pigs as a source of their livelihood. One morning when they woke up, they discovered that all their hogs and pigs were gone. Not knowing what else to do, they went all through the woods hog-calling but still, they couldn't find them. Finally they spotted some mash from which they made corn liquor and following the trail, they located the animals. All the pigs and hogs had gotten drunk. Somehow the farmers managed to get them home.

'Now Frances,' Fannie Lou said, 'If you ever have a boyfriend who drinks too much, get yourself some vinegar and rub him down. We just rubbed those pigs down and sobered them up.'

* * * * * * * * * * * *

SOUTHERN EXPOSURE

"Through Actors' Equity, we took *A Raisin in the Sun* to southern colleges where we set up a producers' contract whereby the drama groups at the colleges worked until I got there. Then we would put the play together, and tighten up our production. I could play the lead and direct the last two weeks. A very exciting experience, it was the first time we had that kind of contract.

"During the run of the play, the grandmother of the young man who played the lead traveled from Louisiana to see the play and afterwards she wanted to meet me. She said what I thought was the best compliment I've ever had in theater and one for which I have always been grateful. 'You know one thing, Miss Williams,' she said. 'I always knew what you were saying between the lines.'

"The home of Fannie Lou Hamer, Mississippi is a beautiful state, the flowers, the foliage, just beautiful. It should be all in harmony, unfortunately, it isn't. The president of the school and his wife, both of whom were white, lived on the campus in an elegant two-story house supported with pillars.

"One day the president's wife came to me and said, 'I belong to a Baptist group and I'd like to have you speak to them.' I accepted gladly. 'Are there many Blacks in the group?' I asked.

'Oh, No. We don't do that.'

178

'You mean you want me to speak to a segregated group? Oh no! I don't do that.'

'Oh dear, we need you so much, what can we do?' She thought for a while, then she said, 'If I invite some of the Black staff from the college, would you do it?'

'That makes sense,' I said. 'In the meantime, give me some pamphlets about the organization so I can see what its function is.'

"She brought me some publications and on them I discovered the name Carrie Meers. Carrie once worked with Sue Bailey for the YWCA many years ago when they were trying to integrate the Y's. After school at night they would sneak to different houses and have integrated meetings. Sue later married Howard Thurman who became the head of the theology department at Yale.

"When I saw Carrie Meers's name on the board of this publication for the Baptist church, I called her in New York. I told her the predicament. She said, 'Frances, if anybody can do anything about this, you can.'

'What can I do?' I asked.

'The organization they head up is in the county. What you can do is set up one in Jackson, not far from there and it will be over theirs.'

"That's exactly what I did. I organized an integrated chapter of this woman's Baptist auxiliary of churches that would be over hers and anyone could join.

"When I spoke at a meeting for the women's auxiliary, the room was filled with well-groomed ladies in suits with matching hat, gloves and shoes. After the talk, a woman whose sister was Catholic related the priest's sermon on the topic of Civil Rights. 'He has the best answer,' she said confidentially. 'Don't go too far to the left or to the right. Just stay in the center of the road. God is with you.'

'This is a beautiful state with all its gorgeous trees and flowers,' I responded. 'I was just wondering what would happen if God had said, 'Let's just go halfway.' There wouldn't be any flowers. There would be a whole state full of stems.' The image was so shocking, everyone took a breath. Out of that kind of moment, I was able to get other auxiliaries set up in Mississippi.

"I was assigned to a little apartment on the campus, and I told the students that any free time I had was theirs. This is something I do on all the campuses I lecture. That way I feel I have an opportunity to exchange ideas and share information about other parts of the world. My apartment was always filled with students.

"At that time, we were fighting very hard for the vote in Mississippi. At intervals, several white students came to the college and they, too, visited my apartment. We talked about the voter registration drive going on. They related what they had observed when they went down to register. When Blacks who were very intelligent, went in to register, something would always be found wrong in their papers. However, when the whites would go to register, all they had to say was, 'abcdefghijk...' or 'hickory, dickory, dock. The mouse ran up the clock.' The whites always passed.

"The black students said that once while they were waiting to get the opportunity to register to vote, some white people decided to paint the building. As they painted they threw paint on the people who were waiting to register.

"After our conversation, I could see how horrible the situation was. Now we have more African American elected officials in Mississippi than in any other state in the country. However, at that time we had nothing.

"When I lectured to the school, it was set up in the chapel on campus. Afterwards, the students told me this was the first time anyone had directed a lecture to them. Prior to my coming, visitors to the school only spoke to the faculty, never to the students. I felt my responsibility was to the students, not to the administration or the faculty, hence I always insisted students be present.

"Two of the heads from a little school in Piney Woods, Mississippi, drove up to Tugaloo in their chauffeured automobile to see the play. They were black with very fair skin. After the performance, they asked me to come to lunch with them and speak to their students. They agreed to provide transportation.

"The day came and as we drove to Piney Woods, I was

amazed to see so many black children with long blond braids and freckles. On the edge of town, stood a huge white barn with double doors. I learned later that the black man who had painted the barn had been lynched because he had painted it white. Once again I was reminded that I was indeed in the deep south.

"Upon arrival, I was escorted into the lunchroom where it had been arranged for a group of young people to sing spirituals for me. When they'd finished, I felt empty and dissatisfied as I got up to speak. 'I don't think the person who taught you those spirituals taught you anything else, because there were overseers with whips and dogs and horrible masters who took advantage of the black woman.' I described slavery as I knew it.

'That's what those spirituals mean. Let my people go! Let us get out of this mire we find ourselves in with no vote and no nothing, working from sun up to sun down, almost have to tell a man when to scratch.' I told them never to sing those songs again, 'unless you think about what they mean.' Then I went on with my speech.

"When I had almost finished speaking, I received a note. 'Dear Miss Williams,' it said. 'Will you allow us to sing for you again after your speech?' They sang again after I spoke and along with everyone else in the room, I cried. I'm still crying.

"Piney Woods School had an immaculate library. On the wall were pictures of African Americans photographed by Carl Van Vechten. I knew all but a few. When I asked the graduating class who came with me into the library how many of the photographs they knew, they admitted they didn't know any of them. 'Would you like me to tell you about them?' I asked. I told an incident that happened with each of the people in the photographs. The students were delighted. They asked if a private room could be set up so they could talk to me. That's when I discovered they were not allowed in the library.

"I heard them whispering, 'Did she say yes?' I turned to the dean and asked what was going on. 'They've been praying every night that you would come and teach a class in theater,' she responded. Then they took me around and showed me some of the most beautiful buildings on campus. One building with a balcony, gorgeous French windows and doors, would have made a lovely little theater. I was very tempted to stay, but I had just come back from Europe and had been in a play on Broadway; I just couldn't do it.

"After leaving Tugaloo, I played several other colleges, and had enriching experiences. Many times in the middle of a scene, never having had such an experience before, the young actors and actresses would break down and start crying. It was moving. Going on campus and working with the young people made me realize too, that I had so much to give and how much was still needed.

"A short time after I had been invited to dinner in Jackson, Mississippi, at a house next door to Medger Evers, he was shot and killed by the Ku Klux Klan."

23

———

MAZATLAN

Frances's brother, Bill, retired from the Post Office in Cincinnati, closed the bowling alley and restaurant, and came out to Los Angeles to stay with her. After working a few years for the Board of Education in Los Angeles, he retired and began going to Sid's Cafe on Exposition Blvd. Jase, a retired postman, had taken over the Creole restaurant. Not having anything else to do, Bill would go there, and if the place needed sweeping, Bill would sweep. If the dishes were piled up, he would wash them.

Bill spent so much time at Sid's, getting drunk or whatever and driving home. Every night Frances worried whether he'd get home safely; it was a strain. Finally, she told him, "We can't live like this the rest of our lives." She knew she had to get him out of Los Angeles. She'd always loved Mexico, having visited there from time to time throughout the years. It was close enough whereby she could fly back and forth to Hollywood in a matter of hours, and far enough away from the hectic life in the states.

She had bleeding ulcers. The doctors said she needed an operation immediately. After being on the board of Actors Equity for twenty years and fighting with those people who didn't believe anything she said, she was not surprised. Whenever she told them what was what, they'd deny it, and two weeks later, implement it. This was distressing and very difficult to take.

"Let's go there and see how we like it," she suggested one evening. To her amazement, Bill readily agreed. So they began to make preparations for the big move. There was so much that had to

183

be done before they could get away; she would have to rent out the house. In addition, she had to go back to New York to take care of some theater business.

Four weeks later, they were on their way to Mexico. A friend drove them down to the border, they took a taxi across, got on a bus and rode across the country. With no particular destination in mind, they boarded the train.

The train traveled across the most gorgeous canyons she'd ever seen. At intervals it would stop near places where the passengers could buy fresh fish from fishermen who cleaned and fried them for their dinner. They journeyed through a place called the Ponderosa with its lush growth of ponderosa pine, and across cattle country in the northern part of Mexico. At one stop, they visited one of the last places Pancho Villa had lived. His wife had turned one part of the house into a shrine. In another part, she sold books, serapes, coats and vests.

For several weeks Frances and Bill traveled all over Mexico finally stopping at a hotel in Mazatlan. Their room had a balcony facing the ocean. That night around midnight a storm came, and the lightening flashed. Bill rushed in from his room waking her. "Sis, you've got to see this." She joined him on the balcony where, in silence, they watched the storm rage over the ocean. When it finally stopped, a sense of peace and well-being washed over her. Bill turned to her, "Sis, Don't you think we've pioneered enough? Let's just stay here."

They rented a lovely three-level house in Mazatlan, Mexico. It was about half a block from the ocean. It had a yard with three banana trees and other kinds of fruit trees, a garden area surrounded by a wrought-iron fence and a manicured lawn.

Bill couldn't speak much Spanish, but he could communicate. A gregarious person, it wasn't long before he could go down almost any street in Mazatlan and everyone knew him. As for Frances, she felt freer than at almost any other time in her life. Living in Mazatlan, made her know how cluttered life was in the states.

Her life, which had always been rich, became even richer.

Without the clutter, she found there was no end to what she could do. Though she traveled back and forth between Hollywood and Mazatlan, Frances, the organizer, organized fashion shows at the big hotels for her new friends, Roberta and Luis who owned a boutique.

She managed a restaurant when the owners had to go out of town. One Easter, she started an Easter egg hunt which she hoped to make an annual event. She studied Spanish and photography at the Instituto Allende, and made many friends as well as kept up her friendships with those in the States who from time to time came down to visit. And because she did so many wonderful things with the children, she planned to buy a big house and make it into a children's theater- similar to the Natalie Satz Theatre in Moscow - and train the children. Neither she nor her brother Bill envisioned their return to the U.S. on a permanent basis. She even considered selling her house in L.A.

* * * * * * * * * * *

One day, she received a call from Louise Patterson who asked if her husband, William Patterson, who was very ill, could come and stay with them. Patterson, who wrote *The Man Who Cried Genocide,* had been the executive secretary of the Communist Party. Frances had known him a very long time. When she returned to the United States from the Soviet Union in 1936, she shunned him because she was vexed with his role there. She talked it over with her brother, and they decided it would be nice to have him. So he came down. "Bill Patterson was in a very bad way. He had a swelling near his colon that looked like a watermelon. I put a castor-oil poultice on his stomach, changed his diet, and in less than two weeks, the swelling went down.

"He didn't believe in tea leaf reading but one day, I convinced him. 'Come on,' I said. 'Let me read your tea leaves.'

'Oh, this is foolish,' he protested.

'You're going to write another book, you're going to lecture again, and you're going to dance.'

185

"When I was in the Soviet Union in the 1930's I always called him 'the fair-haired boy of the Communist Party' because he got first choice of everything that came up. I told him about this 'fair-haired business' that had been on my chest for a long time. He took it pretty well.

"After a month, Louise joined him, and they stayed two more weeks. My brother and Louise just did not get along. She was forgetful. Bill would look for something and she wouldn't know anything about it. Then he'd find it on the roof or somewhere where she'd left it, silly things. They had awful head-ons.

"One afternoon as we were sitting down to dinner, my brother who always said grace before he ate, bowed his head. Patterson turned to him and said, 'You know Bill, you insult me because I don't believe in that.' I held my breath and watched Bill.

'I didn't invite you here,' Bill said, 'You asked to come. This is the way I run my house and if you don't like it, that's your prerogative.'

"Patterson started laughing, 'You're right.'

"Before he left, he could jump up and click his heels. He actually wrote a pamphlet while he was there. When he first came down, he was practically whispering, but by the time he left his voice had become full. He could walk several miles a day. In the morning, he'd help me fix food. The man could slice a pineapple faster than anyone I'd ever seen."

* * * * * * * * * * *

"One day, I noticed Bill was acting kind of strange. I have a sculpture of the head of a dancer, Maudel Bass. As we finished breakfast that morning, Bill looked at the head and said, 'Look Sis, you see her tears. She's crying.' She actually looked as if she was crying. I didn't have time to think about it because someone had come to town and we had to take him downtown to complete some legal work.

"Around noon Bill said, 'I feel like going for a swim. I'll set the fire for a barbecue and the coals will be just right by the time I get back. Meanwhile you get things ready.'

"Hours later, when he didn't return, I went upstairs and sat in my big rocking chair. As I rocked, I talked to God. 'If he's been in an accident, I don't want him hurt or suffering,' I said. 'Please take care of him.'

"Suddenly everything became very calm. I knew he didn't have an accident. I knew everything was not as it should be, but I knew he wasn't suffering. After a while I called some friends and told them what had happened. One woman owned a fleet of taxi cabs in the city, and she said she would send all her drivers out to cover the city to find Bill. They found him. Bill had had a heart attack while swimming. He died on his way to the hospital. I know he and God had a big fight. I could just hear Bill tell him, 'You can't take me unless you take care of my sister.'

"Across the street from our house was a wonderful doctor, Dr. Andradi, who had just finished building his house. He had custom-built furniture and a huge round table especially enlarged to accommodate the six members of his family. He had two extra chairs made for Bill and me. Doctor Andradi came over and set a huge roll of bills on the table and said, 'Don't worry about anything.' The doctor and his wife took care of everything that needed to be done, and I didn't see Bill any more until he was ready to be buried.

"Whenever they had a problem several young people to whom I had served as a mentor would come over and we'd discuss it over coffee. When they learned of Bill's death, they came over and actually said to me, 'You've had a problem. Now we want to see how you handle it.' I was all right. A little girl of three brought over her boy doll and put it in Bill's bed so I wouldn't be lonely. The father of another friend of mine came every day and would take me out for dinner and long drives.

"Another dear friend whom I'd met while living in Mexico helped me get through those difficult days. When Bill died, my relationship with Cindy blossomed. Soon after Cindy graduated from Santa Barbara, her father sent her down to Mexico. He had a schoolmate who lived there. Cindy had almost had a nervous breakdown and her father was concerned about her. He felt if she came down to Mexico for a while, she could recover.

"This schoolmate, Bob, was a friend of Bill's and of mine, too. A tiny little thing, Cindy went to stay with him and his wife. I met her at their house, and I liked her very much. While I was there, Bob announced that they had to go north for a few weeks. I invited Cindy to stay with Bill and me. 'Oh no, it'll be nice just to stay here alone,' she said. The next morning they left. Two hours later the telephone rang and Cindy asked if the invitation was still good. She came over and stayed with us. We've been friends ever since. I knew she was right - like an extension of my family.

"When Bill died, Cindy was attending the University of the Americas and I called her. She said, 'I'll be there on the next plane.' She came from Mexico City to Mazatlan and did not leave my side. I had a lot of legal work to do, and she drove me everywhere and translated for me.

"We couldn't bring Bill back to Los Angeles. He wouldn't have wanted that anyway; he loved Mexico. I had an artist make a big shell and put it on Bill's grave.

"A few days later I was walking with Dr. Andradi and I said, 'It's so comforting to have you. You are like a brother to me.' He said, 'Why Frances, I am your brother.'"

* * * * * * * * * * *

The head of Maudal Bass sits on her porch, a large sculpture, almost a foot and a half, with strong features, in clay. Both of our eyes light on the sculpture briefly, and I stare hard at it, to see what her Brother Bill saw, but I see nothing. We are both silent as I feel Frances's emotions even after all these years, the pain and the resolution to go on. It is the day after Christmas. The day before her house was filled with guests coming and going, a tradition, to partake in her cod fish cakes, spoon bread, cinnamon apples, and hospitality. You never know who you're going to meet on Christmas at Frances's.

188

Rosa Parks, Marilyn McCoo, and Billy Davis and many others drop in to spend several hours with her. But it is the day after, and it is quiet. Her body throbs with pain. She is frustrated because while her mind is active, the pain in her body can no longer be willed away. Today she is lonely.

24

_____

INNER CITY INTRIGUE

The Civil Rights Movement was in full swing before Frances left for Mazatlan. She'd flown to Washington, D. C. with Harry Belafonte and Josephine Baker to participate in the 1963 March on Washington.

In 1965, Maya Angelou lived in one of Frances's duplex apartments and Beah Richards lived in the other. "The compound," as they called her home had always been a sanctuary. Each morning before they began their daily activities, they would check the map to find the best route past the National Guard. It was an exciting and creative time, but it was also a painful time.

What became known as the Watts Riot, but was really a rebellion throughout South Central, L.A., had spawned a flurry of activity on several fronts. Throughout the community, theater groups were performing plays written by blacks about the black experience-theaters like Inner City Cultural Center, Ebony Showcase, and her own, the Frances Williams Corner Theatre. She was stage manager of Frank Silvera's theater on La Cienega in Hollywood where James Baldwin's "Amen Corner" was being performed.

At the time Frances was still on the board of Actors' Equity. Several of the white members couldn't understand the reason for the uprisings. Like many who knew little about African Americans and even less about the community in which they lived, these whites were suddenly aware of black existence. Curiosity about this part of the city had suddenly exploded upon their consciousness. They asked

Frances to take them on a tour of Watts.

Because she respected the people of the community, the idea of taking a busload of whites there to sightsee was abhorrent to her. Despite her reservations, she saw the need to address the ignorance on both sides. Figuring that something of benefit might come from a dialogue, if only to open lines of communication, she invited them to her house. "I don't live in Watts," she told them, "but what I can do is invite some of the people from that community over to my house to speak with you."

One evening, the people from Actors' Equity met with several people from the Watts community in her livingroom. She fixed dinner and after eating, they engaged in a lively discussion around the fireplace. Among the Equity members was a very conscientious, elderly white lawyer. Sitting across from him was a lovely young brown-skinned woman who wrote poetry. Looking quite feminine and delicate, she wore a light blue angora sweater with a white pleated skirt, light blue angora socks and the cutest white kid boots with the toe cut out. The elderly man turned to the young lady and smiled; she returned his smile. Then, he leaned towards her and asked, "I would like to know your opinion of what we could do about this situation?" Her face lit up and she said in a child-like voice, "Why there's only one thing to do. Have a revolution!" There was a dramatic pause. Frances chuckled under her breath and thought, "Out of the mouths of babes..." There were no more questions or comments after that.

1965 was a sorrowful time for her. Frances's niece, Lonnie, P.L. and Cora's only daughter, moved to L.A. from Cincinnati because her aunt lived there. Though Lonnie was in her early twenties, Frances felt responsible for her. One of Lonnie's friends was having a birthday party for her three-year daughter. Lonnie went to her friend's home in Watts to make a cake for the party. Because she worked nights, Lonnie thought she'd better take a nap at her friend's before going to work.

After sleeping a few hours, she awoke, rushed to her car, turned her radio to a jazz station and drove to work. Unaware that the uprising had started, she cruised along Central towards her job.

The streets were not cordoned off, but at one intersection, the National Guard had set up a barricade. As she drove along, singing with her radio, she didn't notice when the guards waved her to stop. Suddenly, they pelted her car with bullets. Someone called Frances to tell her that Lonnie was in the hospital. Frances rushed over to the hospital to see her niece for the last time. All she remembered were Lonnie's words, "Aunt Frances, I'm a human sieve." She was the fourth victim to die in the uprising.

* * * * * * * * * * * *

That same year, Dr. J. Alfred Canon, on the faculty of UCLA, invited Frances over and picked her brain about everything he could think of. She figured she must have talked too much because she was one of the people Canon didn't pick to be on the board of Inner City Cultural Center.

Inner City received a grant for three million dollars and on the board of this prestigious committee were Gregory Peck, who was the chairman, and Roman Polanski. They found an old theater on Washington and New Hampshire and began remodeling it. The Bard, as it was called, had been owned by Thrifty Drug.

A very dear friend of hers, Jim Allen, a construction engineer, was in charge of the remodeling - refinishing the stage and installing toilets and showers in the dressing rooms. One day Frances stopped by to talk to him. Some of the white members of the committee were having a meeting about how the grant money would be used. This peaked her interest.

She overheard one person say, "Three million dollars. Now you know niggers aren't ready to spend that much money. They aren't used to that. We'll have to do something about that."

The board hired a producer and director. Though Frances was not on the board, being a community activist, she became involved.

"A meeting was held in my kitchen, and it was decided that I should get two hundred or more people to audition for parts in plays they contemplated doing.

"I arranged for space at UCLA on Conte Blvd., and set up auditions for three hundred actors. Setting it up for ten people is a big task, but when you have to set up for hundreds, have them on time, ready to be interviewed, and moved on, that was no small task. We auditioned two hundred and twenty-five people, but not one was hired.

"Later I learned that the board brought out thirty actors from New York, along with their wives, children, dogs, and their maids, and rented homes for them with swimming pools in the valley. The only black artist who came out with them was Marilyn Coleman. She didn't have a home or a maid offered her.

"Since the building at Washington and New Hampshire would not be ready in time, they rented another theater to do Moliere's 'Tartuffe,' a period piece. It had been quite evident that they didn't want me on the board; in fact, they wouldn't give me a job doing anything. However, I was very interested in the project since C. Bernard Jackson, the Executive Director, was a friend of mine, and the money was to be used to build a community theater. For this reason, I wanted to know what was really happening, and the only way I knew was to work backstage. Knowing they couldn't refuse, I asked to work on costumes and wardrobe.

"The costumes had to be cleaned at least once a week. Because the damned ruffles were basted on, not stitched, I had to resew them every time they came back from the cleaners. Every night I had to tie up corsets, sew on ruffles and lace up shoes; it was dreadful. After one or two weeks of this, I called the producer and the director and said, 'This is a lot of foolishness and I'm not going to do it anymore.' I told them I wanted the wardrobe woman to come and sew the ruffles on.

'We'll call a meeting with the front office and see if we can come to some kind of solution to this,' the producer said.

'I have the solution,' I said. 'Get the woman to sew on the ruffles. She's being paid enough to do it.'

"Shortly after, they called a meeting at the theater with the wardrobe woman. In front of the producer and director, I laid the

194

woman out, gracefully, but well. The wardrobe mistress began to cry. 'I've never been talked to like this before in my whole life.'

'Well, darling,' I said. 'You've had a new experience. Now you dry your tears and take these damned ruffles and get them sewed.' Afterwards, the director and producer said to me, 'We would pay to have that meeting over again. It was the best performance we've seen in a long time.'

"The men in charge of finances for the theater cleaned Inner City out of a lot of money. If they were allowed to go on, I knew they would ruin the project. So I did something I had never thought of doing before. Every night when I came home, I made notes of what went on in the dressing rooms backstage. I told Jack [C. Bernard Jackson] what I was doing, and he had his secretary transcribe my notes. When we got ready to present these bastards with what they were doing, the words were so accurate, they were theirs like they had spit them out of their mouths. The men could not deny them. As a result, both the producer and the director were forced to resign. It was a new experience for me, but I never regretted doing it for a moment.

"A few days before they were to leave, the wife of the director came to me and said she and her husband had enjoyed working with me so much. 'Since you're such a good organizer, would you organize the farewell party for him?'

'I'd be delighted,' I said. The party was very successful, and for me, an excellent climax since I had engineered getting them out of the job. Others were still in positions working on future plays, but they knew they were on their way out.

"The actors at Inner City and their understudies wanted to organize as a group. At their meeting they said even though I was doing wardrobe, I was still an actress, and a member of the union; They voted me to be an officer in their group.

"Several black actors joined the company. Among them were Roscoe Lee Brown, Paul Winfield, and Glenn Thurman. They began doing plays that featured African Americans in prominent roles. For example, when we did 'Glass Menagerie,' it was the first time a black man played the part of the lover. All the other characters were white.

"In another play, Roscoe Lee Brown was cast in a period piece in which he wore a bulky costume, so bulky he was not able to move in it properly. They told him to wear it anyway. He told me, 'I gave them the fatal blow. I told them if they didn't fix it, I'd tell Frances about it.' He knew it would get fixed, and it did.

"Vinnette Carroll came out from New York to direct a play at Inner City Theatre. She made her directorial debut with a Christmas play written by Langston Hughes, about the birth of Jesus. It was a terrible play, but some of the music was quite good. They did everything but have Jesus on stage. Lang had written me a note asking me to bring all my amen friends to the production. From that time on, this young woman joined the dramatists' guild, studied everywhere she could, and turned into one of our finest directors.

"When Vinnette Carroll began to direct one of the plays, she was so unhappy. Jack asked me if I would go into the theater while she was directing and help ease the emotional conflict she was experiencing. I went into the auditorium and asked her, 'Would you mind if I sit and watch you direct?'

'You're welcome anywhere I am,' she said. 'But first of all, I want to know how you get along with these white folks?'

'There are ways, and there are ways,' I said, understanding her dilemma. I sat down at the back of the theater and watched her direct.

"She was so upset, almost in tears as she worked. These people were horrible. Whatever she would tell them to do, they'd question it, or simply ignore her. When there was a break in the rehearsals, I went up to her and said, 'Honey, all you need is some pigs feet, greens, cornbread and sweet potato pie. I have some at home. I'll warm it up and bring it to you.' I got into my little car, drove home and brought back the food piping hot. After that, she was a different person. She needed somebody who talked like people; somebody who cared. We all need this. She did a very good job and taught us all a great deal."

Despite the fact that Inner City had become more responsive

to the creative needs of the community, Frances was not altogether satisfied. Part of her dissatisfaction stemmed from the fact that neither her friends C. Bernard Jackson nor his wife Josie were of the community. He was an excellent musician who had written some very fine plays, and she, a great woman, but both were not from the grassroots of the community. Though they did an admirable job, it was difficult. The advantage Frances felt she had was that she was interwoven into the community. She was a part of it.

(At her memorial, C. Bernard Jackson related several encounters he'd had with Frances and how he came to be involved with Inner City. The first encounter was when Frances called him to direct a play written by Maya Angelou and starring singer Ketty Lester. Though he was a musician, he agreed to do it. The second encounter was when Frances called him after the Watts Rebellion and told him, "Jack, you're going to start a cultural center...dedicated to serve the needs of the underserved. It's time!" Again, he said, he agreed as he and Alfred Cannon had been discussing it for some time prior. The third encounter was when he was the recipient of the Frances Williams award.)

25
———

WOMEN'S CONFERENCE/ WORLD PEACE COUNCIL & AFRICA

During the mid to late 1970's and into the 80's, Frances was actively involved in local, national, as well as international issues. On the local level in 1979, she represented the Coalition for Black Trade Unions on the Police Crimes Tribunal Grand Jury. The Jury held a mock trial set up for the purpose of informing and constructively motivating the community on the issue of police brutality and its use of deadly force against members of the community. It sought to address the killing of unarmed citizens from Leonard Deadweiler in 1965 to Eulia Love in January of 1979.

Other members of the Grand Jury were William Steiner, National Lawyers Guild; Rev. Philip Zwerling, minister of the First Unitarian Church of L. A.; and Rev. Al Dortch, Chairman of the Coalition for Economic Survival. The trial was held at Fremont High School and, due to careful planning, was successful in meeting its objective. (Sat. Apr. 29, 1979 SCLC *The Legacy Newsletter*)

In 1976, Frances was co-chairperson along with Rev. Al Dortch of the United Front for Justice in South Africa. Two years later, she urged the formation of a local chapter of the National Anti-Imperialist Movement in Solidarity with African Liberation (NAIMSAL) which was headquartered in New York and had close ties with the African National Congress. The Los Angeles Chapter of NAIMSAL became one of the first groups to picket the South African Embassy in West L.A. In 1978 she traveled to Chicago to help form Women for Racial and Economic Equality (WREE) and in

1986, she helped to organize the Art Against Apartheid, a group of committed artists, who performed in schools around Los Angeles to inform students about Apartheid in South Africa.

In addition, Frances traveled to Moscow, Greece, Cuba, Suriname, and to Lisbon, Portugal as a representative of the World Peace Council. For a woman in her 70's, and even then suffering from severe pains in her left leg which was diagnosed as "tubercular cocsitis in the arthritic stage," she was remarkably active.

"In 1975 I was preparing to go to the Women's Conference in East Berlin, Germany when the president of the World Peace Council said, 'Frances, why don't you stop by Brussels on your way. They're having a meeting on Africa that I think you should attend.' I had a general knowledge of Africa, but I didn't really know it the way I would have liked.

"Meetings were held all day long and most of the night. What disturbed me was that there were all these white people who seemed to know the answer to Africa's problems. It irked me that I didn't know enough about Africa to refute them. They talked a lot about Namibia and Angola. They said the MPLA was the group to support. I thought, 'How in the hell do these white people know about this and I don't. How can they tell me which group I should align myself with in my Africa!' The third day they asked me to sit on the stage. I felt like a fool because I didn't know enough about Africa. We talked, and they must have felt awfully sorry for me because I felt sorry for myself. This whole experience shook me up because it showed great holes in my knowledge.

"From Brussels, I went to East Berlin for the women's conference. A fourteen-women steering committee held a panel discussion. Sprinkled among a number of the groups were lesbians who I'm sure were members of the CIA. One woman on the steering committee was so disruptive it was difficult to make progress.

"At dinner one evening, the women from South Africa told us their technique for resistance which was so illuminating. They were clear in their objective and they were doing a good job. It strengthened me a great deal to see these militant women who were ready to take a stand whether they were inside the country or outside.

"After a group meeting, we had an open meeting with all the women. We were a little late getting there because we were talking to the South African women; therefore, I had to sit at the back of the auditorium. Each person was allowed twenty minutes to present her problem to the general committee. We gave more than twenty minutes to the woman on the steering committee who had been so disruptive earlier. She harangued for almost an hour. I thought, 'What would my South African friends do in these circumstances?' "I walked to the front of the auditorium and right up to this woman and in my Ethel Waters voice I said, 'Bitch, Go to your room!' She sputtered, 'I don't have to...' 'If you don't go, I won't be responsible for what happens to you.' A few of her friends came up and said, 'You don't talk to her like that.' I turned to them and said, 'You go, too! We don't need any of you here. You've had time, now go to your rooms!' They left.

"I don't know what I would have done, but I would have done whatever was necessary to get the results we had to have. Many days after I overheard people say, 'There she is.' Some young women wrote poems about me. After the incident, the chairperson of the steering committee came up to me and said, 'Oh Frances, I'm so glad you're on our side.'

"A few nights later, a group of us went to a club in East Berlin. Someone invited this very handsome dark brown-skinned man, a physician, to sit at our table. Being an actress, I can tell what you're saying when I can't understand the words. He said in another language, 'I'll not sit down with any goddamn Americans.'

"I waited until I got near him and I said, 'I want you to know that I'm fighting just like you whether you want to sit with me or not.' He grabbed me in his arms and kissed me, apologized and said, 'Order anything you want.'

"Shortly after I came home, I received an invitation from the World Peace Council to go to Angola for their first independence day celebration. I was the only American representative in Angola for that independence celebration. Several of the others were from other

MEET IT, GREET IT, AND DEFEAT IT

European countries including Brussels.

"The parade, lasting from early morning until evening, was spectacular. Everyone participated carrying whatever they had. All the people who belonged to any of the unions marched with their tools. Painters marched with paint brushes and pails, construction workers carried their tools. Children with one shoe on, children with their father's or mother's shoes on marched.

"Every morning before taking us to various parts of the country, people from different areas of the government would lecture to us for two hours, preparing us for what we were going to see. Then each day we would visit a different part of the country - one day to the east coast, next day to the west coast. In the northeastern section where there was oil, the guide said to me, 'If you want to know who owns us, look at the names on the doors.' Inscribed on the office doors were names like Brown, Scott, White, so American, I thought. Angola was a member of OPEC.

"Situated on acres of land was a huge, unbelievably beautiful building with a gorgeous rose garden. Just below the building was a parkway that ran right to the ocean. Inside the building were banquet rooms with mahogany or cherry wood tables that when the sliding doors were removed fit together making one long table. The tables, elegantly set, were filled with platters of seafood, bread, wines. Never had I sat at a longer table.

"To think that these Portuguese bastards had been living in style on the backs of the Angolan people! When Angola got its independence, the Portuguese left taking everything they could except their Mercedes. Throughout the three weeks of my visit, I had one at my disposal.

"I stayed at one of the newer hotels. The rooms were large and beautifully planned. In my bathroom I counted seven to nine snow white heavy Turkish towels with the name of the hotel engraved on them.

"On the spur of the moment, we requested to be allowed to visit the southern border where we hoped to look over into Namibia which shares the border with Angola - the southern boundary of Angola

202

is the northern boundary of Namibia. The country is lush, and during the fight for independence, getting food across was difficult because the bridges had been burned.

"When I got off the plane, at the far edge of the field, I saw one of the strong fighting groups of Angola, the whole contingent of fighting women. They wore red tee shirts and full skirts with a print of Agostinho Neto stenciled in black, red, orange and white. To see these women, knowing what they had to go through to keep their families together and to be on the pecking line with their babies on their backs and rifles in their hands - I was so moved!

"All my life, something crazy has happened to my legs, but when I saw them, I ran until I reached those women and hugged and kissed every one. We cried together, we laughed together. Though we didn't speak the same language, we understood each other. Every fiber of my being was affected by this experience.

"From the airport, the group was escorted to the center of town and asked to go up in the tower and speak. A number of people understood English. We spoke, but what astounded me was the number of people present on such short notice. Thousands lined the street to greet us.

"The Cuban soldiers were there, too. They knew why they were there and accepted their responsibility. They told us how long they had been away from home, and what it meant that they could help another country right the wrongs that had been done to them over a period of time. Before the Portuguese left, we were told, they ripped out parts of the apparatus needed to refine sugar. I met Cuban soldiers who knew how to replace those parts. Their contributions were invaluable.

"Across the border, in Namibia, were mansions where the people in power had lived, and behind them were shacks much like the plantation houses and slave shacks in the South. The people who lived in the shacks had raised the landlords' children from infancy to adulthood. The people in power were so frightened when the Namibians who reared them communicated to each other in song, they took them up to a ravine, lined them up, shot them and pushed them over into the ravine. Ironically, a hundred feet from this ravine was a gorgeous sculpture of Jesus.

"The next morning after we'd had our schooling, the president of the People's Republic of Angola, Agostinho Neto, sent for us. A poet, Neto had also been a surgeon and had had to perform operations in the bush. He wanted to hear our thoughts about what we'd been exposed to. In the presence of this great man who was doing so much for his people, I was so awed, I was almost intimidated. No one spoke so he turned to me and said, 'Miss Williams, I know you have something to say. Our women have all fallen in love with you and they've sent you a gift.' They had presented me with yardage of the material they used for their skirts.

"That evening was Agostinho Neto's birthday. The theater was filled to capacity; with both sides opened to allow those who could not get in to see and hear the festivities. Each of us was asked to write a paragraph. Not knowing at the time that Neto was a poet, I wrote a poem.

"Actually I didn't know it was a poem until the head of the World Peace Council read it and said, 'This isn't just a statement, it's a poem.'

"Miriam Makeba was among the guest. I found out she was staying at the country house with Augustinho Neto's mother. When she came on the stage with her musicians, you felt she looked into the eyes of every person in the auditorium. She didn't say a word, it was so deeply moving. I'd never encountered anything to that degree until the woman from the army came to see me at the hotel.

"We got up early every morning, had breakfast, listened to a lecture before taking trips to see the country, and we came back in late afternoon. One day we had the afternoon free. My energy level was low because of the mad pace we'd been going. I thought, at last I can get some rest. I was just stepping out of my door when I got a call telling me that a woman from the army was downstairs and that she wanted to speak with me. I was hungry, tired, and I'd anticipated doing very little. I asked if she'd join me in the dining room for lunch. She said she'd join me but she didn't care for anything to eat.

"This woman was one of the heads of the army. We greeted one another and before she said anything, she looked at me from head to toe for almost twenty minutes and said not a word. She gave me the kind of look Miriam Makeba had given the audience at Neto's birthday party. This woman wasn't about to speak to me until she knew who I was. I was as gracious about it as I could be.

"When she finished her twenty minute inspection, she said, 'I can talk to you.' She told me about her father who had been so militant and had helped so many people to escape. Each time they tried to capture him, he'd escape. When they finally did, they not only killed him, but they cut him into little pieces so that they'd know he couldn't be put together again. Fortunately, her brother escaped to the United States.

"She told me how President Neto and his mother, who was a school teacher, taught in the bush. Because the shacks the people lived in were constantly being burned down and had to be rebuilt, in order to give the children an education, they had to find security in the forest. The closest thing to this experience, I remembered, was what happened to the Irish. They, too, had to teach their children in the bush.

"One day we planned to go up the river. To get into the boat which sat several feet below, we had to walk on a rickety wooden wharf and climb down into it. I didn't know quite how I'd get into the boat, but I knew I was going to go. Finally, I jumped up, kicked my feet out behind me, and landed on the rump of my behind. My toes barely touching the rim of the boat, I managed to scoot inside.

"Over the weekend we were invited to President Neto's country home. Once again we took a boat. The boat was enclosed with portholes to see out. I sat beside President Neto's mother, and we had a ball. We talked and laughed about everyone on board. We ate couscous, chicken, seafood and shrimp that she had prepared. Miriam came up beside me and whispered, 'Look Fran, I've lived with her all day long and she doesn't speak any of the languages I know, and I don't speak Angolan, so all we do is stare at each other all day long. I want to know what you're talking to her about when I know you don't speak her language.' I couldn't explain. All the way up we were communicating with each other, we understood each other.

"One night they gave a gorgeous banquet for us on a court, with cemented floor, a huge space. At one end was a table of stone surrounded by pillars where the president sat with his guests. As I sat down, the president sent over his daughter to say he had a place for me at his table. I joined them. How they had taken what little they had and made so much of it amazed me. All they had was seafood, but it was fixed in so many stylish ways.

"I was very impressed with the young people of Angola who were given appointments with the government. So often, they said, they were tired after their schooling and doing their chores, but whenever Neto called, everything stopped until they could fulfill whatever he needed. Because so many doctors had left the country during the fight for independence, when I returned to the states, I got together a group of six doctors from New York to go there."

* * * * * * * * * * *

"The following year, Earl Robinson and I attended the World Peace Council in Athens, Greece with Jules Dassin and his wife Melina Mercouri, who was the Minister of Culture. I'd worked with Jules Dassin at Actors' Lab when he directed *The Birthday* about thirty years earlier.

"At the program were 15,000 people. The people went up in the hills and brought back laurel wreaths which they presented to me and other delegates. One of the meetings was held at a big civic center. The auditorium was packed. I sat in the first row hugging the stage.

"People from about seventeen different countries got up and spoke telling about the horrible things the U.S. had done to their country. I was so embarrassed I wanted to hide the tears that ran down my face. I felt like standing up and saying 'I'm an orphan, please claim me. I don't want to go back to that place.'

"The next morning I had to get some pictures made and a

very fine man came by to take me to the photographers. As we were driving to the photographers, he said, 'Miss Williams. I looked at you last night and you looked ill. I wondered if you could go this morning.'

'How could you see?' I thought because I sat so close to the stage that no one could see my face.

'I looked.'

'I was so ill after hearing what the U.S. had done that I didn't want to claim that I'd belonged to the U.S."

"A few days later, I went to see the Bishops who were noted for the very tall, impressive looking hats they wear. Gathering up my courage, I went up to one and said, 'I want to greet you from the working people of the U.S.'

"He looked at me and said, 'I accept. If you had not said the workers, I would not have accepted.'

"I feel that every artist must have political training. They must know the working people of this world. Since I became an actress-activist, I have never separated life from art."

26

FRANK'S PLACE

In the middle 1980's, after appearing in over 40 films, and a host of television shows and commercials, Frances was presented with a part in a new series entitled, *Frank's Place*, a role that Charles Champlin described as "a plum assignment to crown a career that has lasted more than seven decades." (*L.A. Times*, Oct. 18, 1988) The series would evolve around a man who inherits his father's restaurant and bar. He travels to Louisiana to see the place for the purpose of selling it before returning to his Boston home and work. However, after a brief stay, he becomes attached to the people there and decides to remain and build the business. The assortment of characters ranges from a beautiful mortuary owner, a wise bartender, a self- effacing white lawyer, to an outspoken young waitress and a cleaver-wielding head cook. The oldest living waitress is Miss Marie who dispenses wisdom and advice garnered from her years of living.

A casting agent called Frances's agent who sent over the script for *Frank's Place*. She read it and loved the part of Miss Marie. This was far different than the script she'd received for her first Hollywood film role forty years earlier. When she received the script for *The Magnificent Doll*, mailed Special Delivery, she searched through the entire script several times and was so hurt because the role of Amy, the maid, was so sparse and one-dimensional.

Times certainly had changed. The character of Miss Marie had something she could work with - something more than the stereotyped characters that Hollywood films were filled with. In fact, all the characters on the show were well-rounded and likeable even some of the villainous ones.

Tim Reid and Hugh Wilson, the producers of *Frank's Place* had been friends for many years having both worked on *WKRP in Cincinnati*. Reid knew Frances from the time she coached Marilyn McCoo and Billy Dee and checked scripts for their summer television series. At that time, Reid and Jay Leno were trying to get into television. Both worked on the show as stand-up comic relief.

At the initial audition for *Frank's Place*, Frances read for Hugh Wilson. When she finished reading the script, she said to him, "This must have been written by a black person," because she said, "I felt it captured our essence so well." He smiled. It was one of the greatest compliments he'd ever received, he said, and "I want you for the role of Miss Marie."

Another audition, the major one to finalize the casting, was held several days later in a big studio at CBS. When she learned that Hugh Wilson was not going to be there, she was perplexed. How could the producer/writer not be at this important audition? She learned later that he had made up his mind about who he would cast for the roles and had decided that if CBS did not accept his recommendations, the show would have to go on without him.

"I'd heard of shows ruined because the people who made important decisions didn't know what they were doing, so I understood his determination."

Frances walked into the huge auditorium and the first thing she noticed was the number of young people in decision-making roles. Having had many years of experience, and having worked with all sorts of people, she was a little surprised, and skeptical. They looked much too young to know what they were doing. The room was crowded with people waiting to audition. When her turn came, she read the script and when she finished, she heard a voice from the back of the crowd. It was Tim Reid. He came over and greeted her warmly. A few weeks later, she got a call from her agent saying she'd gotten the role of Miss Marie.

The first episode she liked very much, but the second, she didn't. In fact, she decided that the script was going to be changed

210

or she would no longer be a part of the cast. That was the first big challenge. The script called for a scene in which Frank befriends a common alley cat named "Jesse Jackson." Frances was angry. To belittle one of the important African American leaders was an affront. First she called Wilson. When she explained her annoyance, he said, "I don't see anything wrong with it." "Well, I do. Jesse Jackson is our hero and if you don't mind doing that to someone we respect, why don't you just call the cat Jimmy Carter?" she said, and left it at that. Next she called Tim Reid who was in Chicago at the time. He said, "Hold everything until I get back." The cat was renamed, and Frances remained with the series.

"Yet, in spite of that, we became a family. I hadn't been there for more than two or three episodes when Daphne and Tim invited me to their home for dinner. After the third episode, Tim called me into his office and thanked me for helping us become family. How people honestly feel about one another shows. Unless everyone becomes family, I find it difficult to work."

Once when Frances helped set up *Amen Corner* at Frank Silvera's theater, the cast was at each other's throats. Off stage no one spoke to anybody without hostility. Everyone acted as if they wanted to kill each other. To go into this and have to get it together was going to take a lot of effort, she felt. A Belgium woman who was living with her at the time taught her a lot about foods. She taught her about brown rice and told her how it had been used in prisons to change the disposition of the prisoners. It had also been used in Africa to cure a sickness there. Frances decided to try it on the actors at the theater.

In one scene of *Amen Corner*, that called for the family to sit down to dinner, Frances set up the meal using variations of brown rice. To her delight, her experiment worked. Soon, the bickering stopped; the cast gelled so well, when the play was taken to New York, it got rave reviews.

"I didn't do that with *Frank's Place*. Instead they all learned to work together, showing that they cared for each other as persons rather than just doing our job."

MEET IT, GREET IT, AND DEFEAT IT

Frank's Place captured the folk experience of African Americans in New Orleans better than anything on television ever had. With plausible plots based on Black life, veteran actors, an integrated cast and production staff, it was quite revolutionary. Above all, it had quality. Some people in New York saw *Frank's Place* when it opened and called to say that in all their lives they thought they'd never seen a play that portrayed blacks with such dignity and quality as that series. Roscoe Lee Brown told Frances his phone was constantly ringing with people talking about the series and saying how lucky they were to get it on.

In a 1987 interview with Drama-Logue magazine, Frances says of the series, "We don't have to be ashamed of it, you know? And I have great pride in being a part of it." She characterizes Miss Marie as "the core of the culture of Louisiana...I think Miss Marie's role is to get people back to the original culture. She has stuck with the old things and is a part of it. And they respect that at Frank's Place."

Fan mail from across the country came pouring in praising the show, with many letters addressed to Miss Marie, including a marriage proposal, letters from whites as well as blacks. In one letter to Frances, the writer says, "You are a vital and effective force in the show..." Another says, '*Frank's Place* ' is something you can always be proud of."

When the show was cancelled, everyone was disappointed. Once again letters flooded the network executives in protest. One letter, indicative of many, noted the fact that the show was moved around so much, it couldn't find an audience. CBS debuted *Frank's Place* on Monday night for a special showing and was supposed to switch to Saturdays where it would compete with NBC's comedy lineup. A few weeks into the season, Nielsen ratings, the first from the new people-meter system, noted that *Frank's Place* had dropped "from 27th overall to 29th with females 18-49, and was 34th among male viewers 18-49." CBS moved the show to another time slot, then to another night. This reshuffling did little to build the show's audience. Some of its devoted followers gave up trying to reschedule their viewing habits to fit CBS's capriciousness. One fan characterized CBS executives as "not dealing in good faith or that you hoped to deliberately confuse and discourage people." Frances was very disappointed but, in her typical fashion, she picked herself up, dusted off her Birkenstocks and moved on.

27

EPILOGUE

REAPING THE HARVEST

At the memorial, one person after another recited anecdotes of their relationship with Frances and the effect she had had on their lives - the advice she gave one, the phone call she made to a studio executive to open doors for another, the work she did at SAG and Actors' Equity on behalf of minorities. Even her resignation speech to the TVA board was read. The celebration ended with the children who lit candles and sang.

Frances was like a conductor. She guided you to a station and you took it from there if you had the guts. On the one hand, she was always encouraging you, prodding you along, making you extend yourself whether you wanted to or not. On the other hand, Frances could be a hard task master, critical, manipulating and demanding. "She could be so overpowering that people would choose to take other avenues or courses to achieve their goal." (Admiral Dawson, interview with the author, August 1996)

Her good friend, Libby Clark said, "[Frances] was the consummate actress, on stage at all times. You knew she had a tremendous ego, but you weren't offended by it. I called her 'Star.' I'd say, 'Frances, are you on stage today?' (Interview with the author, July 1996)

Despite her shortcomings, all agreed that Frances's role in the struggle against injustice was crucial. She now resides with so many of our unsung heroes, like Charlotta Bass, Louise Brooks, Bill Taylor, and Rose Chernin.

MEET IT, GREET IT, AND DEFEAT IT

One time I asked Frances her views on life in general and her own life in particular. She thought for a while, her gaze tracing the flight of a blue jay just outside her window. It landed on a branch of the fig tree in her yard. Her eyes then darted to a butterfly that flittered around her Bird of Paradise nearby. She smiled and said, "When racism is involved and it affects people, we must be alerted and we must stand and fight where we are, be creative in our fight and not dodge it. We must accept and do it. Even though you think you don't matter, you must do something about it. My favorite saying 'meet it, greet it, and defeat it,' comes to mind. If you do this, life is much more interesting. And you feel good...

"So many times we get to the door and don't have the courage to turn the knob and go in. I'm sure there are many more steps after that. Whenever I used to give a speech, I'd always say, 'Meet it, Greet it, and Defeat it.' But then it struck me that if we just meet it, greet it, and defeat it, we will always be at the level of our enemy. My desire for our struggle is to reach, and go beyond the last reach to be a part of the whole picture. As I thought it through I realized that you can't just accept the level at which people put you. You must be free enough to go beyond that.

"I have regretted nothing I've ever done. I have often wondered how it would affect my ability to get jobs, and I think it has made a difference, but I didn't know enough about it to know that it did. It's like those who say 'we were very poor, but we had so much love in our family, we didn't know we were poor...'

"From time to time, people would come and urge me to move to Hollywood but I told them, 'You don't need me there. If I moved there I'd just bring you whatever happens in Hollywood. My contribution is to bring you what is happening in my neighborhood. The only way I know what is happening is to live there. Almost every week I had this fight.

"Then one day, a little girl's grandmother came to me. Her husband had a big barbecue business on the east side. The grandmother had been rearing this child who was about 5 years old. The grandmother said, 'My husband died and I don't know what to

216

do.' I told her I would help her. 'That's what my granddaughter said you'd do. She said, 'Don't worry. Ms. Williams lives right up the street and she'll help you.' I organized the funeral, wrote telegrams, made long distance calls, dissolved the business, I was needed. That this child knew that I was there told me I was right in my decision.

"One of my favorite stories is one about the children on the street. They had a bench outside and one day I had given them some cookies and had gone back into the house to work. I heard them talking. A little Asian boy asked his friend, 'Tell me, who do you like best, Frances or Santa Claus?' I thought, 'By God, I made it!' The little girl just over two who lives next door said, 'Frances, you're a mess. But you're me's mess.'

"My decision was confirmed that if the children could see that they needed and wanted me, then I was glad I was here. It's proven all through my time here, I'm still in that little house and things are still decided around that old kitchen table."

A Partial List of Frances E. William's Acting Credits

FEATURES

Lying Lips - 1939, Micheaux Film Corp., Oscar Micheaux dir.
The Notorious Elinor Lee - 1940, Micheaux Film Corp., Oscar Micheaux dir.
Magnificent Doll - 1946, Universal, Frank Borzage dir.
The Reckless Moment - 1949, Columbia, Max Ophuls dir.
Three Secrets - 1950, Paramount, Robert Wise, dir. Showboat - 1951, MGM, George Sidney dir.
Man with a Thousand Faces - 1957, Universal, Joseph Penney dir.
Together Brothers - 1947, Fox William A. Graham, dir.
River Niger - 1976, Cine Artists, Krishna Shah, dir., Ike Jones Productions
Sparkle - 1976, Warner Brothers, Sam O'Steen, dir.
Piece of the Action - 1977, Warner Bros., Sidney Poitier dir.
The Toolbox Murders - 1978, Cal-Am, Dennis Donnelly dir.
Uncle Joe Shannon - 1978, United Artists, Joseph C. Hanwright
The Jerk - 1979, Universal, Carl Reiner dir.
The Glove - 198-, Pro International, Ross Hagen dir.
With Just a Little Trust
Cross Creek - 1983, Universal, Martin Ritt dir.

TELEVISION - 1970's - 1980's

<u>Series</u>

The Waltons - Lorimar
General Hospital - ABC
Gibbsville - Columbia Pictures
Magic Carpet to Fine Arts - Children's TV Series, NYC
Hill Street Blues

Designing Women
Frank's Place
The Boys
Police Story
The White Shadow
Freestyle - KCET
Palmerstown
Little House on the Prairie
Hill Street Blues

Movies for Television

A Dream for Christmas
A Woman Called Moses
King
Sister, Sister
Ambush Murders

Stage

You Can't Take it With You - *on Broadway and on tour*
A Raisin in the Sun - *on Broadway and on tour*
Little Foxes - *on tour*
Male Animals - *on tour*
Scarlet Sister Mar - *on tour*
Amen Corner - *Hollywood*
Taming of the Shrew - *Hollywood*
Abe Lincoln - *Hollywood*
(About 65 others)

BIBLIOGRAPHY

Blakely, Allison. Russia and the Negro: Blacks in Russian History and Thought. Washington D.C.: Howard University Press, 1986.

The California Eagle Newspaper, May 20, 1948.

"Ceramics by Tony Hill." Ebony Magazine. Nov. 1946.

Evett, Marianne. "Karamu House, A Multi-Cultural Dream Come True." *Plain Dealer Magazine* [Cleveland], Sept. 1990. 18+

Foner, Philip Sheldon. Organized Labor and the Black Worker, 1619-1980. New York: Praeger, 1974.

Hughes, Langston. *I Wonder as I Wander.* An Autobiographical Journey. New York: Thunder's Mouth Press, 1956.

The Legacy Newsletter. SCLC, April 29, 1979.

Los Angeles Sentinel, Newspaper. Jan. 1946, March 1946, August, 1948, Oct. 1948.

New Theatre Magazine. July, 1936.

Vose, Clement E. *Caucasians Only.* Berkeley University of California Press, 1959.

The World Magazine. May 1976.